CAMBRIDGE
ENGLISH
for schools
Workbook One

ANDREW LITTLEJOHN & DIANA HICKS

CAMBRIDGE
UNIVERSITY PRESS

PUBLISHED BY THE PRESS SYNDICATE OF THE UNIVERSITY OF CAMBRIDGE
The Pitt Building, Trumpington Street, Cambridge CB2 1RP

CAMBRIDGE UNIVERSITY PRESS
The Edinburgh Building, Cambridge CB2 2RU, United Kingdom
40 West 20th Street, New York, NY 10011-4211, USA
10 Stamford Road, Oakleigh, Melbourne 3166, Australia

First published 1996
Fifth printing 1998

Printed in Italy by G. Canale & C. S.p.A. Borgaro T.se (Turin)

ISBN 0 521 42173 X Workbook
ISBN 0 521 42169 1 Student's Book
ISBN 0 521 42177 2 Teacher's Book
ISBN 0 521 42181 0 Class Cassette Set
ISBN 0 521 42130 6 Workbook Cassette

Contents

1 Welcome to English!

1 Word puzzles

1.1 Find the words

There are 10 words in the puzzle.
They go down (↓) and across (→).

```
F  C  A  R  S  W  I  M
O  J  I  A  A  E  W  G
O  K  Q  D  N  H  M  K
T  L  W  I  D  R  P  T
B  Y  R  O  W  Z  I  E
A  R  I  O  I  T  A  I
L  T  E  N  C  A  N  G
L  W  J  L  H  X  O  H
M  U  S  I  C  I  E  T
```

1.2 Your puzzle

Make a puzzle for your class. You can make:

   a letter square (see Exercise 1.1)

or a word puzzle

Find a long English word. For example: TELEPHONE

Put a word through each letter. Put a number on each word.
Write the word in your language or draw a picture. For example:

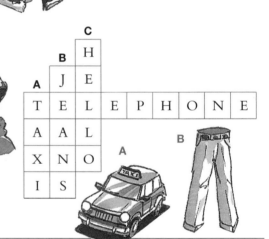

2 Misfits

Introductions

Join the head, body and legs of the children.

1	2	3	4	5
Hello! My name's Daniel. I'm eleven years old. I live in Green Street. I can play football very well.	Hello! My name's Fiona. I'm ten years old. I can play the piano very well.	Hello! My name's James. I'm twelve years old. I can swim very well.	Hello! My name's Susan. I'm thirteen years old. I live in Park Road. I can ride a bicycle very well.	Hello! My name's Sam. I'm nine years old. I live in Long Street. I can play the guitar very well.

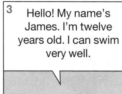

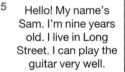

3 Describe your friend

Draw a picture or stick in a photograph.
Write about your friend like this:

This is my friend.
His name is Martin.
He is 13 years old.
He lives in Hill Road.
He can play the guitar very well.

a picture or photograph of your friend

Don't forget the 's'

lives

....

....

....

....

....

4 Talk to David

Write your answers to David's questions.

DAVID: Hi, my name's David. What's your name?

YOU: ....

DAVID: Oh. How do you spell that?

YOU: ....

DAVID: That's a nice name. How old are you? I'm 12.

YOU: ....

DAVID: Which school do you go to?

YOU: ....

DAVID. Do you? I go to Central Secondary School. Where do you live?

YOU: ....

DAVID: Really? I live in Ireland. What language do you speak?

YOU: ....

DAVID: Your English is very good!

 Now talk to David on the cassette.

5   What are they saying?

Fill the gaps.

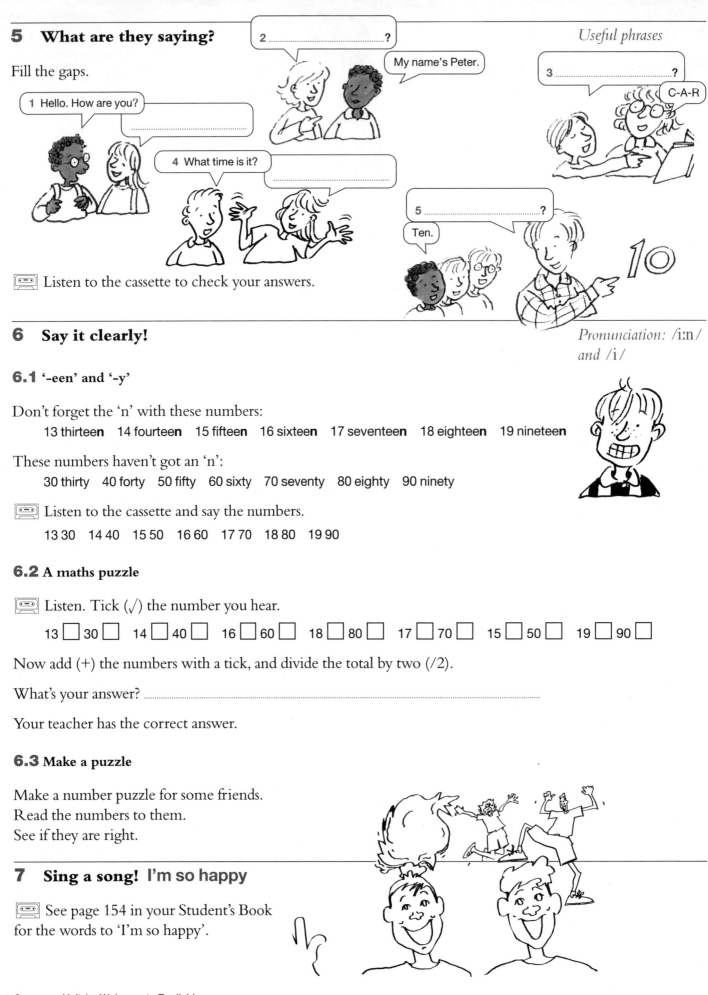

1 Hello. How are you?

2 ....?

My name's Peter.

Useful phrases

3 ....?

C-A-R

4 What time is it?

5 ....?

Ten.

📼 Listen to the cassette to check your answers.

6   Say it clearly!

Pronunciation: /iːn/ and /i/

6.1 '-een' and '-y'

Don't forget the 'n' with these numbers:

13 thirteen   14 fourteen   15 fifteen   16 sixteen   17 seventeen   18 eighteen   19 nineteen

These numbers haven't got an 'n':

30 thirty   40 forty   50 fifty   60 sixty   70 seventy   80 eighty   90 ninety

📼 Listen to the cassette and say the numbers.

13 30   14 40   15 50   16 60   17 70   18 80   19 90

6.2 A maths puzzle

📼 Listen. Tick (√) the number you hear.

13 ☐ 30 ☐   14 ☐ 40 ☐   16 ☐ 60 ☐   18 ☐ 80 ☐   17 ☐ 70 ☐   15 ☐ 50 ☐   19 ☐ 90 ☐

Now add (+) the numbers with a tick, and divide the total by two (/2).

What's your answer? ....

Your teacher has the correct answer.

6.3 Make a puzzle

Make a number puzzle for some friends.
Read the numbers to them.
See if they are right.

7   Sing a song!   I'm so happy

📼 See page 154 in your Student's Book
for the words to 'I'm so happy'.

2 Extension Around the world again

Choose the parts of these optional revision exercises that you need to do.
Look at the Test and Extension exercises on pages 14–21 in your Student's Book.

1 You're in England. Get ready to go!

'To be'; 'have/has got'

1.1 Where are they?

Look at the pictures.
Where are Roger and Maria?
What have they got? Fill in the gaps.

He .... on a submarine.

He .... a hat.

.... on a train.

They .... a lot of books.

She .... on a plane.

She .... a lemonade.

He .... in a helicopter.

He .... a big suitcase.

They .... in a hot air balloon.

They .... two cameras.

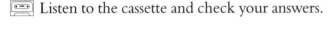

.... in a car.

They .... sunglasses.

Listen to the cassette and check your answers.

1.2 Talk to Linda

Write your answers to Linda's questions.

LINDA: Hello.

YOU: ....

LINDA: My name's Linda Collier. What's your name?

YOU: ....

LINDA: I'm English. Are you English?

YOU: ....

LINDA: I'm thirteen years old. How old are you?

YOU: ....

LINDA: I live in Manchester. Where do you live?

YOU: ....

Now talk to Linda on the cassette.

2 Stopover in America!

2.1 At the airport

📼 Talk to the man at San Francisco airport.

MAN: Welcome to San Francisco.

YOU: ....

MAN: Can you tell me your name please?

YOU: ....

MAN: And your telephone number?

YOU: ....

MAN: OK. Thanks. Your address?

YOU: ....

MAN: And your first language is ...

YOU: ....

MAN: How old are you?

YOU: ....

MAN: Thanks. Bye.

2.2 A suitcase label

Write on your suitcase label.

NAME ....

ADDRESS ....

TELEPHONE NUMBER ....

NAME OF SCHOOL ....

COUNTRY ....

AGE ....

---

3 Stopover in Australia!

3.1 Where are Darwin and Alice Springs?

Read about some places in Australia.
Where are Darwin and
Alice Springs on the
map – A or B?

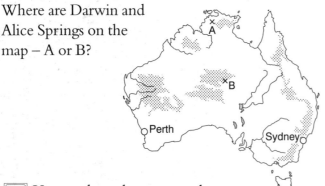

📼 You can hear the texts on the cassette.

3.2 Your town

Write about your town on another piece of paper.
Write about the buildings, the people, and the weather.

Alice Springs is in Australia. There are 23,000 people in Alice Springs. There are big farms near this town with cows and sheep. Some people look for gold here. It is very dry here in the winter and the summer. There are mountains and rivers near Alice Springs. It is not near the sea.

Darwin is in Australia. There are 75,000 people in Darwin. It is a big port. Many ships come to this town. There are a lot of tourists in the winter and the summer. They go to the big National Parks near Darwin. There are a lot of trees near the town.

4 Stopover in India!

Negatives

4.1 True or false?

Look at the map of India. Are these sentences true or false?

True   False

1 India isn't a very big country. ☐ ☐
2 India has got a lot of deserts. ☐ ☐
3 There isn't a railway in India. ☐ ☐
4 There are a lot of big towns in India. ☐ ☐
5 India isn't near Pakistan. ☐ ☐

Key

▨ Desert
⋯⋯ Railway

PAKISTAN Delhi NEPAL Calcutta INDIA Bombay Hyderabad Bangalore Madras SRI LANKA

N W E S

0   1,000
km

4.2 True/False sentences about your country

Write some true/false sentences about your country.
Give them to your class next lesson.

5 Stopover in Pakistan!

*Adjectives;
'have/has got'*

5.1 On the telephone

▭ Talk to Ahmed on the telephone in Pakistan.

AHMED: Hi. How are you?

YOU: ....

AHMED: What do you look like? I've got brown eyes. What colour are your eyes?

YOU: ....

AHMED: Have you got long hair?

YOU: ....

AHMED: I've got straight hair. Have you got curly hair or straight hair?

YOU: ....

AHMED: Can you send me a picture?

YOU: ....

AHMED: I've got a lot of homework tonight. Talk to you soon. Bye!

YOU: ....

5.2 A description of Ahmed

Write a description of Ahmed.

Ahmed has got black hair and ....

....

....

6 Welcome back to London!

6.1 What are the places?

Join the description of the cities to the correct place on the map.

1 This is Rome. It is the capital of ___Italy___ .
They speak Italian there. Three million people live in Rome. Rome has got many beautiful buildings.

2 This is Lisbon. It is the capital of ....
They speak Portuguese there. One and a half million people live in Lisbon. Lisbon has got a big statue on the mountain.

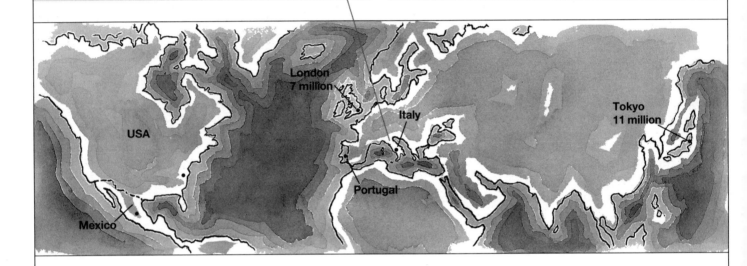

3 This is Washington DC. It is the capital of .... They speak English there. About one million people live in Washington. Washington has got many important offices.

4 This is Mexico City. It is the capital of ....
They speak Spanish there. Twenty million people live in Mexico City. Mexico City has got an important museum.

Listen to the cassette to check your answers.

6.2 Write about London and Tokyo

London (England); 7 million; English; Buckingham Palace
Tokyo (Japan); 11 million; Japanese; The Meiji shrine

3 Topic Around our school

1 What's the word?

Put the words under the pictures.

Three words are missing.
What are they?

offices flats river houses
airport bus station

offices

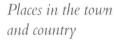

Places in the town and country

2 Places in a town

Reading

Read the sentences and look at the map.
Write the correct number in boxes a–g.

1 There is a train station in the north west next to the school.
2 There is a swimming pool in the south west next to the train station.
3 There are factories in the south east next to the market.
4 The bus station is in the north east next to the shops.
5 There are a lot of offices in the south west next to the school.
6 The old castle is in the north east next to the park.
7 There is a new hospital in the south east next to the factories.

3 Read the letter from Alice

Read the letter from Alice.

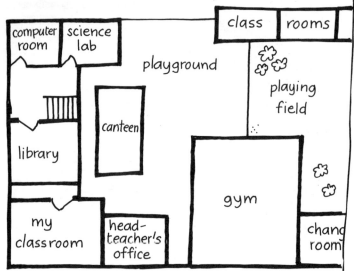

Dear everyone,

Here is a map of my school. It's not a very big school. It has got about 400 students. My classroom is next to the headteacher's office! Near my classroom there is a big library and the canteen. A lot of students have lunch in the canteen. I don't have lunch at school. I go home at 12.30.

The computer room is upstairs next to the science lab. We don't have our lessons in the science lab but we go to the computer room on Tuesday for computer lessons. I like computers.

After school we play in the playground outside. My friend Tim plays football on the playing field next to the playground. He is in the school team. I am in the school basketball team. We play basketball in the gym. Write and tell me about your school.

Best wishes
Alice

You can listen to the letter on the cassette.

Draw a plan of your school. Write to Alice. Tell her about your school.

Dear Alice

Here is a plan of my school.
The headteacher's office is ...
The school library is ...

Best wishes

4 Say it clearly!

/æm/ *(am)* /aɪm/ *(I'm)*

There are two ways to say 'I am' in English. Listen. Say these sentences.

Yes, I am.   No, I'm not.

Answer David's questions.

DAVID: Hi, are you on holiday today?

YOU: ....

DAVID: Oh! I'm on holiday today. I'm on holiday for eight weeks in the summer. Are you on holiday in July and August?

YOU: ....

DAVID: Really? I'm on holiday in February too. Are you at school then?

YOU: ....

DAVID: Your English is very good. Are you learning English at school?

YOU: ....

DAVID: Excellent! Talk to you soon. Bye!

5 A puzzle

Vocabulary

Read the clues and fill in the puzzle with the words.

Clues

1 I've got eight s.................... on my timetable.
2 My f.................... lesson is History.
3 347 × 284? Easy! I like M.....................
4 My mother works in an o.................... in the centre of town.
5 I've got long hair but my friend has got s.................... hair.
6 I don't like Tuesday b.................... we've got Chemistry.
7 I ride my b.................... to school.
8 I have six l.................... every day.
9 In the morning we have two lessons and
   then at b.................... we have a drink.

What word is in the middle?

6 In the bags

Reading

Read the letter. Write the days next to the bags.

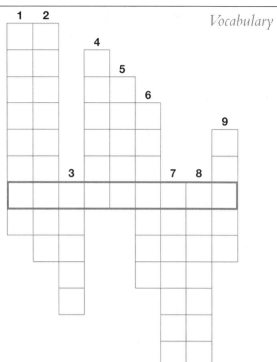

> Dear Everyone,
>   Thanks for the letter. Can I tell you about my week?
>   On Saturday morning I play football with my brother and on Sunday I play the trumpet with my sister. The weekend is great!
>   Monday is school! I have Geography and English on Monday. That's OK. The next day I have History and Biology. I like Wednesday because we have two lessons of Maths and Chemistry. I'm good at Science. Thursday is OK because we have Maths and Physics. I like Maths. On Friday we have music and three lessons of Sports! A lot of my friends like Sports but I don't!
>   Please write and tell me about your week.
>   Love Maria.

1 ....
2 ....
3 ....
4 ....
5 ....
6 ....
7 ....

7 Sing a song! In my town, in the countryside

See page 154 in your Student's Book for the words to 'In my town, in the countryside'.

1 North, south, east or west?

Maps; writing

1.1 A map of Australia

Look at the map of Australia and complete the sentences.

1 Perth *is in the south west.*

2 Darwin ....

3 Broome ....

4 Alice Springs ....

5 Brisbane ....

6 Townsville ....

7 Melbourne ....

8 Sydney ....

1.2 A map of your country

Draw a map of your country. Write about the cities.

1.3 A map of Cheltenham

Look at the map. What is in these squares?

Square	Square
A1 *a river*	B3
A2, B4 and C1	C2
A3	C3 and D3
A4	C4
B1 and D1	D2
B2	D4

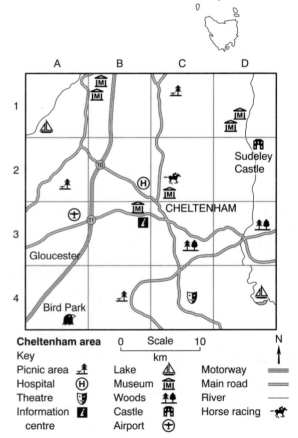

Cheltenham area
Key
Picnic area — Lake — Motorway
Hospital (H) — Museum — Main road
Theatre — Woods — River
Information (i) — Castle — Horse racing
centre — Airport

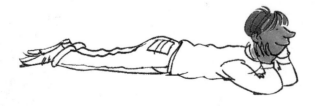

2 An adjective puzzle

Adjectives

Find the adjective in each sentence. Write it in the puzzle.
What word is in the middle?

1 There are many beautiful pictures in this museum.
2 I live in a small house.
3 This is an expensive cassette.
4 Liverpool has got an important football team.
5 Sophie has got curly hair.
6 Her father is a rich man.
7 Ali has got straight hair.
8 It's a very hot day today.
9 I've got a new bicycle.

3 Steve's letter

'don't' / 'doesn't'

Read this letter from Steve.

Read these sentences about Steve. Are the
sentences possible or impossible?

After school Steve plays in the garden of his house.

Impossible! Steve doesn't live in a house.

1 At the weekend Steve goes to piano lessons.

....

2 In the morning Steve's brother goes to school by car.

....

3 After school Steve meets his friends at the swimming pool.

....

4 There is a big farm next to where Steve lives.

....

5 Steve's mother drives the car to work.

....

6 Steve plays football with his friends every Saturday afternoon.

....

Dear Everyone,

Thank you very much for your letter. It is
great to have some pictures of you and
your school. Here is a picture of me in my
flat. Our flat is in the city centre. My
family doesn't have a car. I go to school
on the bus. I have a sister and two
brothers. They go to my school too. I have
lunch at school. I don't like it very much.

After school, I go swimming. I am in the
school swimming team. My friends like
football but I don't like it. I don't have
time to play a musical instrument but I
like to buy cassettes of pop music. Here is
a cassette of my favourite band.

Best wishes,
Steve

4 Say it clearly!

/ð/ (this) /θ/ (think)

There are many words with 'th' in English.
Can you write four here?

....

....

Can you say them?
Listen. Say the sentences.

Put your tongue between your teeth!

This is the Brown family.
They have three children.

This is the father.

This is the mother.

This is Arthur.

This is Elizabeth.

This is Matthew.

5 In the shop

Going shopping

Talk to the shop assistant. Look at the pictures and buy two things.

Excuse me, how much are these jeans?

That's expensive!

How much is this bag?

How much are these jeans?

Can I pay for the jeans and the bag please?

Here you are.

YOU: .... ?

SHOP ASSISTANT: £250.

YOU: .... !!!

SHOP ASSISTANT: They're very good.

YOU: .... ?

SHOP ASSISTANT: They're £15.

YOU: .... ?

SHOP ASSISTANT: That's £4.50.

YOU: ....

SHOP ASSISTANT: That's £15 and £4.50. That's £19.50 please.

YOU: ....

SHOP ASSISTANT: Thank you.

5 Making exercises

1 Look at these exercises

Types of exercises

What do these exercises practise? Match the exercise with the word.

Reading ☐   Vocabulary ☐   Spelling ☐   Grammar ☐

A Put the words in the right order.

1 letter for Thanks your
2 are pictures of Here two me
3 the we got green In have summer a dress

B Read the letter and choose one of the words for each space.

here   tell   letter   friends

T-shirt

jumper   jeans

Dear Sara,

Thanks for your . . . . I can . . . . you about my school clothes. All my . . . . have got jeans. In the summer we can wear a T-shirt and in the winter we can wear a jumper. . . . . is a picture of me in my school clothes.

Love Ali

C Put the letters in the right order.
They are names of places in a town.

facroyt   meumsu   staonit   pakr   scloho

D Read the letter from Sara.
Answer the questions.

1 Sara likes her uniform.
2 There are two uniforms.
3 Sara's uniform is white.

True	Not true	We don't know

jumper

skirt

summer dress

Dear Ali,

Thanks for your letter. Here are two pictures of me in my school uniform. It's green! I don't like it very much. I've got a green skirt and green jumper for the winter. In the summer we have got a green dress.

Love Sara

Compare your answers with other students in your class.

2 Write some exercises

Read the letter and make two exercises.
You can make:

	a reading exercise	*or*	a vocabulary exercise
or	a spelling exercise	*or*	a grammar exercise

Look at the examples in Exercise 1 and the *Ideas list* on pages 150–151 of the Student's Book.

Central Secondary School
High Street
Liverpool

Dear Parents,

This year there are two Sports Days. The first Sports Day is for children from 11 to 13 years old. It is on 15th June at 2pm. The second Sports Day is for children from 14 to 16 years old. It is on 16th June at 2.30pm. All mothers, fathers, brothers, sisters and friends are welcome. There is a parents' race at the end of the afternoon. Have you got your sports shoes?
We have got many different races this year and now the children can play basketball in our new Sports Hall. Parents can play in a parents' basketball team. Please come and watch your children play their sports!

David Bowne

Headteacher

Don't forget to write the answers on the back of your paper! Put your exercises in your class *Exercise Box*.

6 Help yourself with spelling (1)

1 Look, cover, write, check

– *look* at the word
– *cover* it up
– *write* it down
– *check* it

1 Look.

2 Cover.

4 Check.

Practise with these words:

restaurant   library   favourite   different   break

Now find five more words in the *Language
Record* in Unit 3.
Then *look* at the word, *cover* it up, *write* it
down and *check* it.

3 Write.

2 Play a game: Word pairs

1 Take 20 pieces
of paper.

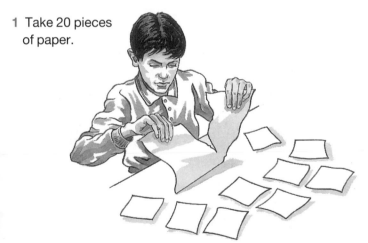

3 Turn the papers over.

2 Find ten difficult words to spell.
Write each word on two
pieces of paper.

4 Test your memory.
Find a pair of words.

3 Spelling groups

3.1 Sounds and spelling

In English one sound can have different spellings.
Look at these three spellings of the sound /iː/:

Write these words in the right circle.

green me tea three
read she teacher

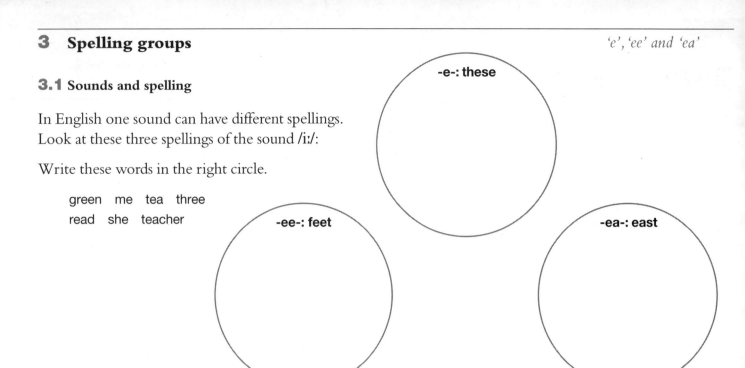

-e-: these

-ee-: feet

-ea-: east

3.2 The missing sound

These words are from Units 1–5. The /iː/ sound is missing.
Write 'e', 'ee' or 'ea' in each word.

fr...............   pl...............se   sl...............ph

tr...............s   j...............ns   s...............

b...............   h...............

Check in your Student's Book *Wordlist/Index* (pages 156–159).
Write the words in the circles in Exercise 3.1.

3.3 A spelling book

Make a spelling book.
Write the words in spelling
groups. Like this:

ee

green
see
sweets
coffee
free

ea

east
please
clean
read
jeans

7 Test yourself

Here are some things from Units 3–6.
How well do you think you can do them?
Put a tick (√) in the box.

Now do this test and see if you are right!

	I can do it:	very well	OK	a little
1	describe your town			
2	say negative sentences			
3	talk about what you like at school			
4	use new words			
5	go shopping			
6	grammar words			

1 A town in Scotland

Read this text about a town in Scotland.

> I live in Perth, a small town in the east of Scotland. It is
> 50 kilometres from Edinburgh. My school is in the north
> west of the town near the river and the train station.
>
> Perth has got a population of 43,000 people. There is a
> big castle in the town centre. A lot of people come to
> visit the castle in the summer. Near the castle there is a
> big park. On Saturday there is a market in the park.

Now write about your town. See Units 3 and 4
in the Student's Book for help.

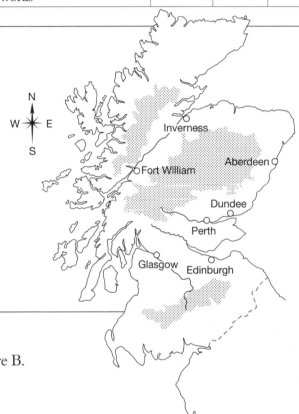

2 Write about picture B

Look at pictures A and B. Write five sentences about picture B.
For example:

> Picture B hasn't got a block of flats.
> There isn't a car in picture B.

3 Linda's questions

Write your answers to Linda's questions.

LINDA: Hi. My favourite schoolday is Monday. What's your favourite schoolday?

YOU: ....

LINDA: Why?

YOU: ....

LINDA: Oh. My favourite subject is Maths. Do you like Maths?

YOU: ....

LINDA: I have Maths every day. When do you have Maths?

YOU: ....

LINDA: What's your favourite day at the weekend?

YOU: ....

LINDA: Why?

YOU: ....

LINDA: Really? I like weekends. I can listen to music all day!

Talk to Linda on the cassette.

4 After school

Reading and writing; using new words

4.1 Linda's letter

Read Linda's letter.

Write the information in the family diary.

> Dear friend,
> Thanks for your letter. I like English and Maths too. We have a Maths test every Friday morning! What time do you finish school? My school finishes at 3.30 and I get home from school at 4 o'clock. On Monday, at 5 o'clock, I have a guitar lesson for half an hour. I am in the school football team and on Tuesday we play football at school with the Sports teacher for an hour. On Wednesday I go

> shopping with my parents at the supermarket. I don't like that very much but I can help in the supermarket. On Thursday I watch television when I get home. There is a good programme about animals on television. On Friday my friend Sam comes to play at my house. We play with the computer in my bedroom. Write and tell me what you do after school.
> Love Linda

Family Diary

Family Diary

Linda: after school activities

MONDAY

TUESDAY

WEDNESDAY — Supermarket with me!

THURSDAY

FRIDAY

SATURDAY

SUNDAY

4.2 A reply to Linda

Write a reply to Linda and say what you do after school.

5 Going shopping

Write the phrases in the speech bubbles.

Bye. Thanks.   Can I have that mask please?   That's expensive!   How much is that mask, please?

Let's try another shop.   Can I have that cloak, please?

Listen and check your answers.

6 Grammar words

Put these words in the correct columns.

rich trumpet years sing small
live chair big know straight
town important address blue
country speak

NOUN	VERB	ADJECTIVE
country	*speak*	*blue*

Now look back at the chart at the beginning.
Were you right?

8 Fluency practice A Parcel of English

1 Read the letter. Find Mrs Tanner, Ben, Tom, Sara and Emma in the photograph. Write their names beside them.

Dear Everyone,

This is a picture of our class. We are in Class 1. The name of our school is Bewsey Road Secondary School. Our English teacher's name is Mrs Tanner. Can you see her in the picture?

Our names are Sara, Emma, Tom and Ben. Can you see us in the picture? Sara has got long black hair. She can play the guitar very well. Emma has got short blonde hair and she can paint very well. Tom has got long, curly hair and he plays football in the school team. Ben has got short black hair and he can speak French very well. He's got a French mother!

Send us a picture of your class and tell us about your group!

Love Sara, Emma, Tom and Ben

Bonjour!

2 Can you do the puzzles?

How many places can you find?

```
U G E U M L I B R A R Y O L
N W E R T Y U A O P C M J F
S T A H I O N I G H A N J A
J U I K L O P R G B S D C C
C D E R F T G P Y B T N J T
S C H O O L S O R T L G H O
V F G T H Y U R J K E J N R
F F I C E T G T S H O P K Y
```

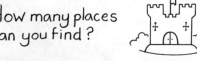

What are the missing words to make a sentence?

Can | us

pic ture

your | school?

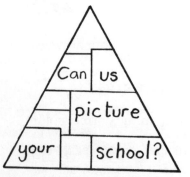

A code! What does this say?

23–18–9–20–5/ /21–19/ /1/ /12–5–20–20–5–18

$a = 1, b = 2, c = 3, d = 4, e = 5, f = 6$, etc.!

3 Read the letters. Mark each person's house on the map of the town.

7 Bewsey Road
Hi everyone!
I live very near my school. I walk to school every morning. I get up at 8.30 and have breakfast at 8.45. I run to school in 2 minutes. Do you live near your school?
Bye Tom

15 Canning Drive
Dear Friends,
I go to school on the bus. The bus stops near the Post Office. The Post Office is near my home. I get up at 8 o'clock. Sometimes I run for the bus. Do you go to school on the bus? Here is my bus ticket.
Love Sara

Single	Bus
45p	013

52 Mornington Street
Hi everyone!
I go to school by car. My mother works in the library near our house and my father works in the centre of town in an office. I get up at 7.45. We are in the car for 20 minutes. There are a lot of cars in the town in the morning. Do you go to school by car?
Best wishes Ben

64 Crosfield Street
Dear Everyone!
I go to school by bicycle. I've got a red bicycle, it's very big and fast. I live near the park so I ride my bicycle to the park and then in Bewsey Road. I get up at 8.15 and ride to school in 10 minutes. Have you got a bicycle?
Bye Emma

4 Read the letter. Can you find Class 1's classroom on the plan?

Dear Everyone,
Here is a map of our school. The headmaster's office is near the front door. The school library is near the headmaster's office. There are four classrooms next to the library. Upstairs there is a Science laboratory. Our classroom is next to the Science laboratory. Next to the laboratory there are two canteens: one for the teachers and one for the students. Opposite the canteens there is a big gymnasium. Outside there is a playground and a big playing field for football. There isn't a swimming pool at my school. Have you got a swimming pool?

Send us a map of your school.
Yours Sara and Emma

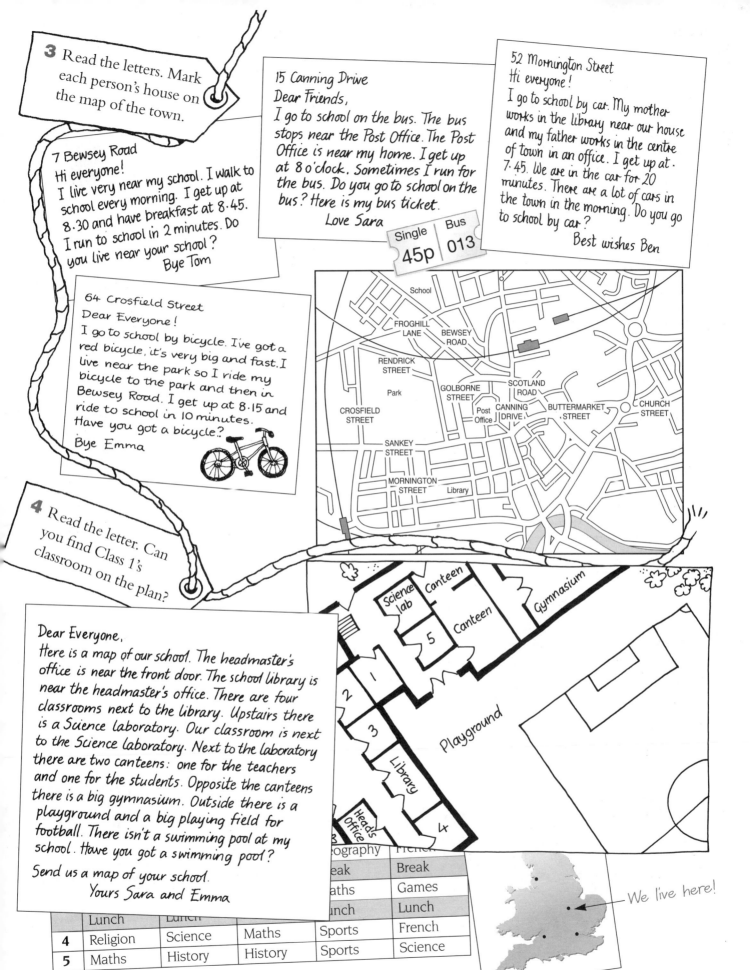

We live here!

	...eography	French		
	Break	Break		
	...aths	Games		
Lunch	...nch	Lunch		
4 Religion	Science	Maths	Sports	French
5 Maths	History	History	Sports	Science

A picture dictionary (1)

Label the picture.

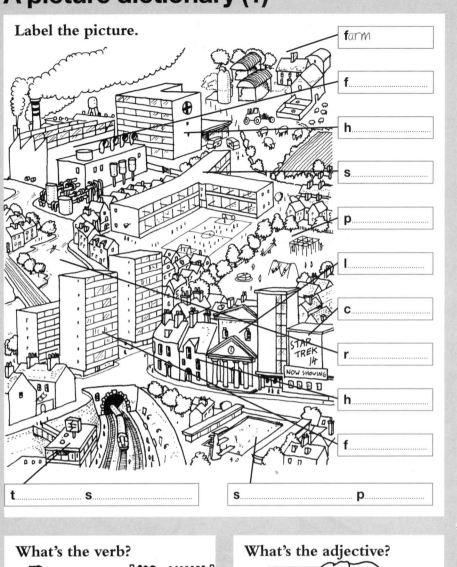

farm
f..................
h..................
s..................
p..................
l..................
c..................
r..................
h..................
f..................

t.................. s..................

s.................. p..................

Write the names of the subjects.

geography

s..................
h..................
b..................
m..................

What's the noun?

people

b..................
t..................
h..................
m..................
o..................
b..................
e..................
h.................. c..................

What's the verb?

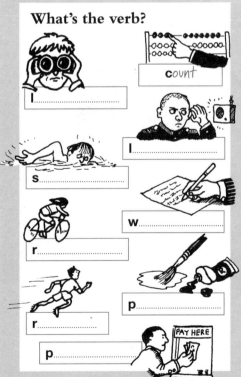

count

l..................
l..................
s..................
w..................
r..................
p..................
r..................
p..................

What's the adjective?

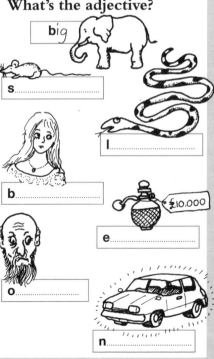

big

s..................
l..................
b..................
e..................
o..................
n..................

9 Topic In the wild

1 Word puzzles

Vocabulary

1.1 Find the names

What animal is it? Join the clues to the correct names in the square. They go down (↓) and across (→). (See page 48 in the Student's Book.)

```
D O G B C E F U E W
P E O P L E R S H S
X E M O G K E Y W H
Z H O R S T F O W E
W C R O C O D I L E
J K P R N K Z C C P
B N C A T J K O O F
E M E F T I R W S D
E H S X E E P N D B
O W E L E P H A N T
```

1 This animal eats meat. It lives for 15 years and it sleeps for 13 hours at night and during the day.

2

3 This animal eats grass. It lives for 20 years and it sleeps for six hours at night.

4

5 This animal eats meat and fish. It lives for 15 years and it sleeps for 13 hours at night.

6

7 This animal eats fruit, leaves and grass. It lives for 60 years and it sleeps for four hours at night.

8

1.2 Make a puzzle

Make a square like the one above for a friend. Write the words across (→) and down (↓).

2 Animal groups

Classifying

Are these animals mammals, reptiles, fish, birds or insects? Put the name in the correct circle.

flies   cats   whales   ostriches   horses   mosquitoes   salmon   dolphins
tigers   bats   crocodiles   lions   goldfish   sharks   flying fish
parrots   monkeys   cows   bees   penguins   rhinoceroses

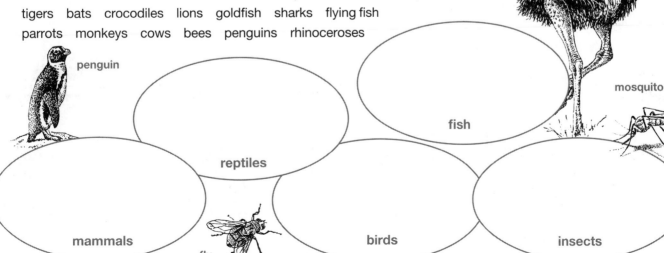

salmon

flying fish

ostrich

mosquito

penguin

fish

reptiles

mammals

fly

birds

insects

3 Say it clearly!

There are three ways to say '-s' in English.

'cat**s**' has an 's' sound   'bee**s**' has a 'z' sound   'horse**s**' has an 'iz' sound

📼 Listen and say the words.

's' sound	'z' sound		'iz' sound
cats	cows	tigers	horses
bats	lions	penguins	ostriches
sharks	dolphins	bees	rhinoceroses
parrots	whales		

📼 Put these words in the correct column. Check your answers with the cassette.

maps   boxes   books
leaves   glasses
shops   rivers   farms
hours   towns   buses

's' sound	'z' sound	'iz' sound

4 Talk to David

Speaking

Write your answers to David's questions.

📼 Then talk to David on the cassette.

DAVID: Hello. My name's David. What's your name?

YOU: ....

DAVID: Have you got any pets at home?

YOU: ....

DAVID: I've got a snake! A long, black snake. It's a python. Do you like snakes?

YOU: ....

DAVID: Well, I think snakes are beautiful. I've also got a cat. His name's Izzy. He sleeps all day. Do you like cats?

YOU: ....

DAVID: What about horses? I can ride a horse. Can you?

YOU: ....

DAVID: What's your favourite animal?

YOU: ....

DAVID: That's my favourite animal, too!

5 Animal reports

5.1 Read and draw an animal

Read the Animal Report about a new animal.
Draw a picture of the animal.

ANIMAL REPORT

Name of animal:	Crocofostfly.
What does it look like?:	It's got the head of a crocodile. It's got the legs of an ostrich. It's got the wings of a fly. It lays eggs.
What does it eat?:	It eats bananas and fish.
How many hours does it sleep?:	It sleeps ten minutes a week.
Where does it live?:	It lives in trees.
How long does it live?:	It lives about a year.

5.2 Write and draw a picture

Draw a picture of a strange new animal. Write about it.

ANIMAL REPORT

Name of animal:	
What does it look like?:	
What does it eat?:	
How many hours does it sleep?:	
Where does it live?:	
How long does it live?:	

6 Sing a song! Wimoweh

See page 154 in the Student's Book for the words to 'Wimoweh'.

10 Language focus

Present simple questions;
possessive adjectives; /s/,
/z/ and /ɪz/; inviting

1 Find the missing piece

Read about humming birds.
Put in the missing pieces.

Humming birds are very ____ animals.
They ____ North America and ____
America. They move their ____ very
fast. They can stay in the same place
in ____ for ____ They drink
from flowers. They also eat small

Reading

Puzzle pieces: a long time · insects. · the air · South · beautiful · live in · wings

▭ Listen and check your answers.

2 Questions

Present simple questions

2.1 What's the question?

Write the full
questions.

Tigers live in Asia. _____	Where do tigers live?
They live for 15–20 years. _____	How long ....?
Tigers sleep during the day and hunt at night. _____	When ....?
Tigers eat meat, including monkeys, deer and buffalo. _____	What ....?
An adult tiger can eat over 50 kgs of meat in one night. _____	How much ....?
Tigers normally have two to four cubs or babies. _____	How many ....?
They live with their mother until they are three years old. _____	How long ....?

2.2 Write some questions

A new student comes to your school. What can you ask?
Write some questions. You can use these words:

dog   cat   swim   chocolate   live
play the guitar   dance   piano
sing   walk to school   paint

Where do you live?
Can you play the piano?
Do you like ...?
Have you got ...?

....
....
....
....
....

3 'my, his, her, your, their' and 'our'

3.1 Fill the gap

1 Is this *your* cat?

2 No, it's .... cat.

3 No, it isn't. It's .... cat.

4 No, it isn't. It's .... cat.

5 It's not .... cat. It's .... cat.

6 It's not a cat! It's .... hat!

3.2 Check that you understand

Write the conversation in your language.

GIRL: When can you come to our house? ....

....

BOY: I don't know. What can we play there? ....

....

GIRL: We can play with my brother's cat. ....

....

BOY: What's its name? ....

GIRL: Tiger. ....

BOY: Have you got an animal? ....

....

GIRL: Yes. I've got a crocodile. His name is Fang. ....

....

BOY: Oh! ....

GIRL: My sister likes Fang a lot. He sleeps in her bed. ....

....

BOY: Ugh! ....

GIRL: Can you come to our house after school? ....

....

BOY: No, I can't! ....

🖭 Talk to the girl.

4 Say it clearly!

Remember the three ways to say 's' in English: /s/ in 'it's' /z/ in 'is' /ız/ as in 'boxes'.

Listen. Write /s/, /z/ or /ız/.

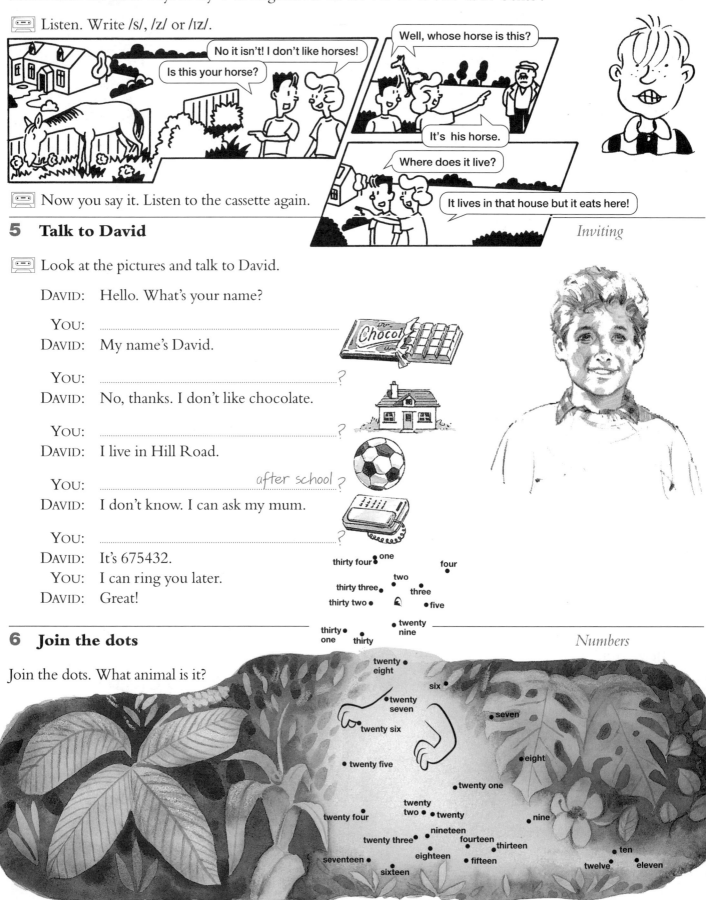

Is this your horse?

No it isn't! I don't like horses!

Well, whose horse is this?

It's his horse.

Where does it live?

It lives in that house but it eats here!

Now you say it. Listen to the cassette again.

5 Talk to David

Inviting

Look at the pictures and talk to David.

DAVID: Hello. What's your name?

YOU: ....

DAVID: My name's David.

YOU: .... ?

DAVID: No, thanks. I don't like chocolate.

YOU: .... ?

DAVID: I live in Hill Road.

YOU: .... *after school* ?

DAVID: I don't know. I can ask my mum.

YOU: .... ?

DAVID: It's 675432.

YOU: I can ring you later.

DAVID: Great!

6 Join the dots

Numbers

Join the dots. What animal is it?

Fluency practice Animal world

1 The missing piece

Find the missing piece
for texts 1–4.

1

This is a giraffe. It is a mammal. It is a
very tall animal. It is over five metres tall.

2

This is a blue shark. It is a type of
fish. They can swim very fast. People can
swim about 6 km an hour but blue sharks
can swim 65 km an hour.

3

This is a firefly. It is an insect. It is a fantastic
animal. There are over 2,000 types of
fireflies but they all do the same thing.

4

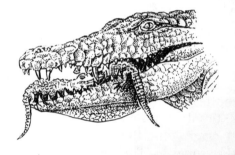

This is a crocodile. Crocodiles are
reptiles. Many of them are very big –
over seven metres. They are the biggest
reptiles in the world.

A

They live in rivers in many parts of the
world. They have short strong legs and
a very strong mouth. A mother crocodile
carries its babies in its mouth.

B

It lives in Africa. It has very long legs. It
is usually white and brown. It eats leaves.

C

They live in many parts of the world.
Many of them are over three metres long.

D

At night, they give light. They have a
small part of their body that shines. They
sleep during the day and move at night.
They eat other small insects.

2   The Monarch butterfly

2.1 Read about the Monarch butterfly

Complete the information on the map.

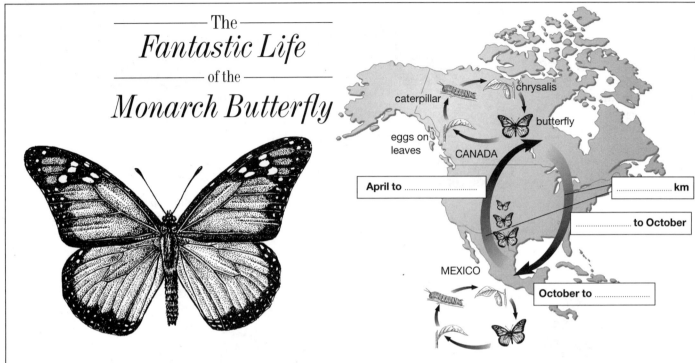

The —
Fantastic Life
— of the —
Monarch Butterfly

caterpillar   chrysalis

butterfly

eggs on
leaves   CANADA

April to ....

.... km

.... to October

MEXICO

October to ....

Every year, millions and millions of Monarch butterflies fly 4,000 km from Canada to Mexico and then 4,000 km back again. They fly 45 km every day for three months. They go to Mexico because it is cold in Canada. They are in Mexico for six months, from October to April. In Mexico, they lay their eggs and then they die. In April, the new butterflies start to fly back to Canada. There, they lay their eggs and then they die. The new butterflies then fly to Mexico. Monarch butterflies always go to the same places in Mexico and to the same trees. How do they know the way? Why do they go to the same trees? Only the Monarch butterfly knows.

▭ Listen to the text on the cassette.

A problem to solve: How long are the butterflies in Canada?

2.2 Talk to a butterfly

Imagine you can talk to a Monarch butterfly. What can you ask?

> **Mr Monarch, why do you go to Mexico?**

1 How many butterflies .... ?

2 How many kilometres .... ?

3 When .... ?

4 .... ?

5 .... ?

12 Help yourself with grammar

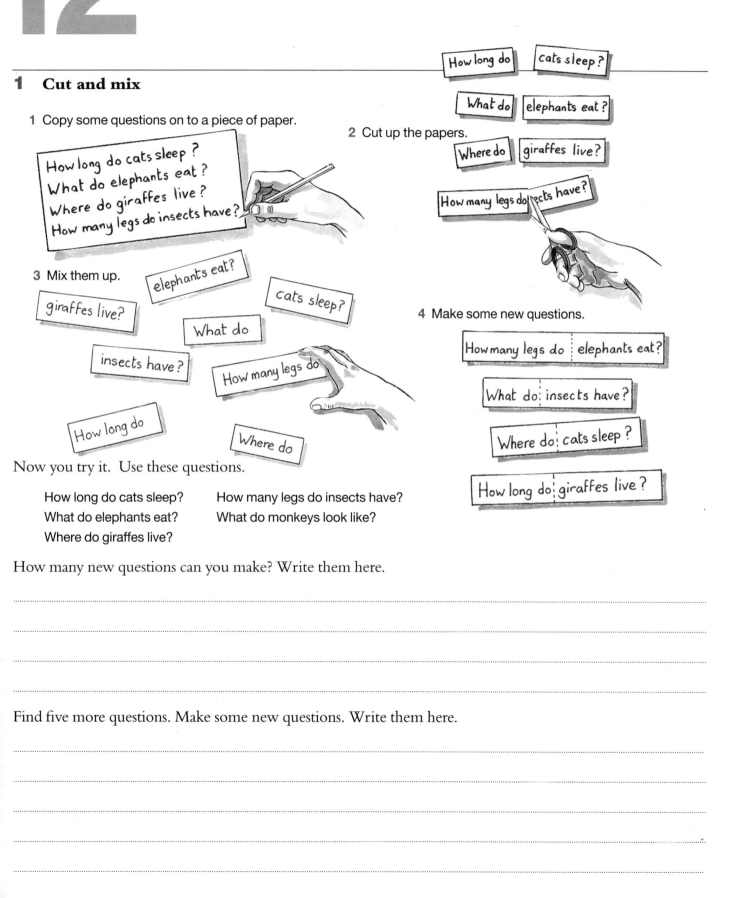

1 Cut and mix

1 Copy some questions on to a piece of paper.

> How long do cats sleep ?
> What do elephants eat ?
> Where do giraffes live ?
> How many legs do insects have?

2 Cut up the papers.

> How long do | cats sleep ?
>
> What do | elephants eat ?
>
> Where do | giraffes live?
>
> How many legs do | ects have ?

3 Mix them up.

> elephants eat?
> giraffes live?
> cats sleep ?
> What do
> insects have ?
> How many legs do
> How long do
> Where do

4 Make some new questions.

> How many legs do | elephants eat?
>
> What do | insects have ?
>
> Where do | cats sleep ?
>
> How long do | giraffes live ?

Now you try it. Use these questions.

How long do cats sleep?   How many legs do insects have?

What do elephants eat?   What do monkeys look like?

Where do giraffes live?

How many new questions can you make? Write them here.

....

....

....

Find five more questions. Make some new questions. Write them here.

....

....

....

....

2   Write your own sentences

Take a sentence from your Student's Book:

Humming birds are very beautiful.

Describe it:

| noun | + | verb | + | adjective |

Write five more:

    1 Giraffes are very tall.   **2** Elephants …   **3** My school …   **4** I …   **5**

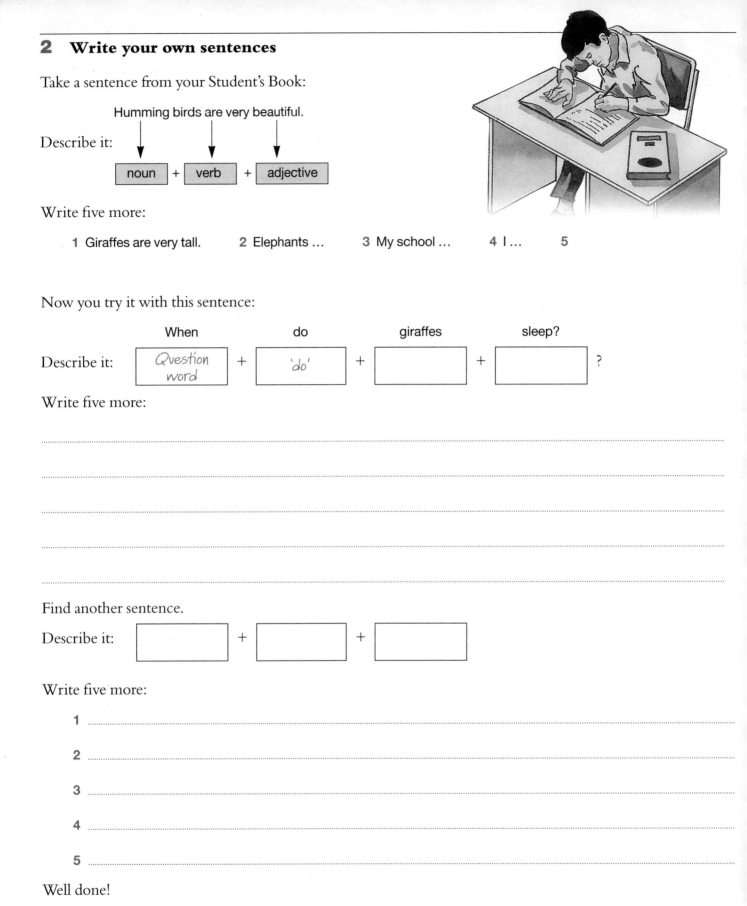

Now you try it with this sentence:

	When	do	giraffes	sleep?
Describe it:	Question word	+ 'do' +		?

Write five more:

....

....

....

....

....

Find another sentence.

Describe it: [   ] + [   ] + [   ]

Write five more:

    1 ....

    2 ....

    3 ....

    4 ....

    5 ....

Well done!

3   Use the techniques

Practise the grammar from Units 1–11 in the Student's Book. Use the two techniques.

13 Test yourself

Here are some things from Units 9–12.
How well do you know them?
Put a tick (√) in the box.

Now do this test and see if you are right!

I can do it:	very well	OK	a little
1 Talk about animals and how they live			
2 Ask for information and invite			
3 'my'/'his'/'her'/'their', etc.			
4 Asking questions			

1 How they live

Read about elephants.

Now write about dolphins.
See Unit 9 in your Student's
Book for some information.

Writing about animals

Elephants live in Africa and India. They are mammals and they are very big. They live for about 60 years. They don't eat meat. They only eat fruit, leaves and grass. They sleep for about four hours at night.

....

....

....

2 Come to my party!

Inviting

There is a new student at your school.
Write your answers and then talk to him. Invite him to your birthday party!

PETER: Hello. My name's Peter.

YOU: ....

PETER: Do you want a sweet?

YOU: ....

PETER: I've got two more friends with your
name. They live near the town centre.
Where do you live?

YOU: ....

PETER: Oh. I don't know that area.
Where is it near?

YOU: ....

PETER: Oh yes.

YOU: (*invite him to your birthday party*)

....

PETER: Yes please! At what time?

YOU: ....

PETER: Great. What's your telephone number?

YOU: ....

PETER: My number is 232675. See you at the
party! Bye.

YOU: ....

3 Meet the family!

Fill the gaps.

2 I sleep in here with .... brother.
This is .... bedroom.
Do you like it?

'my/his/her /their', etc.

1 Hello! Let me show you .... house. You can also meet .... family.

7 This is .... car. It's .... first new car.

3 My sister sleeps in here. This is .... bedroom.

6 We have two dogs. They sleep here in the garden in .... little house.

4 My parents sleep in here. This is .... bedroom. Shhhhh! We have a new baby. Look! He sleeps in .... bed in .... parents' bedroom.

5 We also have a cat. It sleeps in .... bed!

4 What is it?

Asking questions

Here is a very strange animal.
What questions can you ask about it?
Write down six questions.

What .... ?

Where .... ?

How .... ?

Why .... ?

When .... ?

How long .... ?

Ask your teacher next lesson. He/She has the answers!

Look back at the chart at the beginning. Were you right?

A picture dictionary (2)

Label the animals.

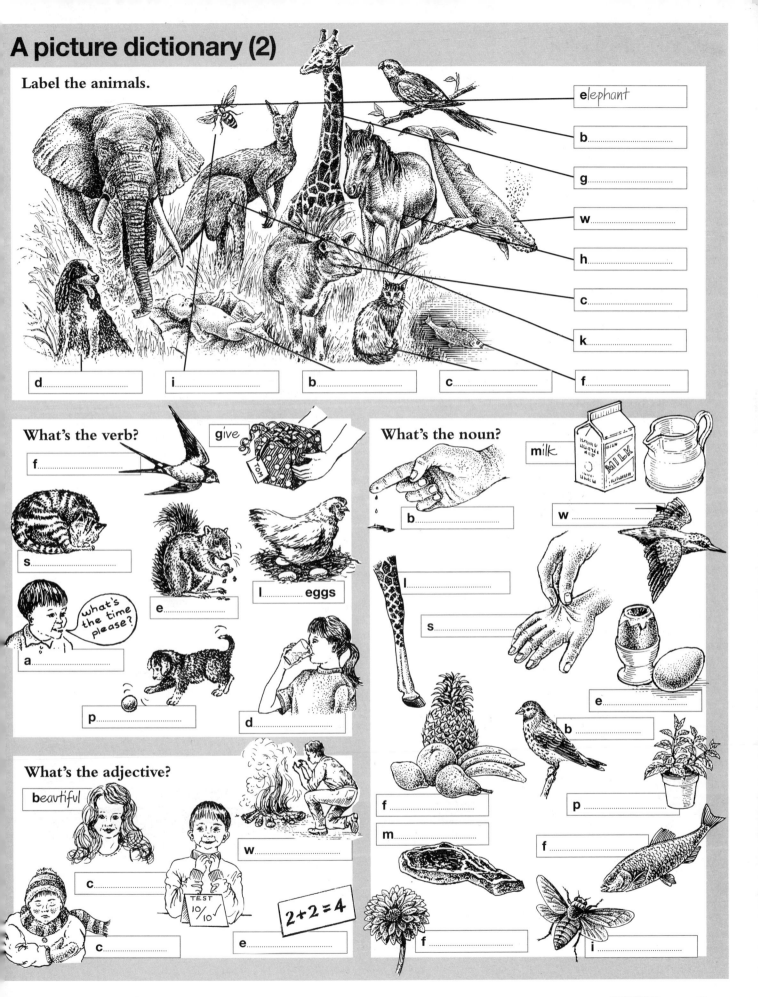

elephant	
b....................................	
g....................................	
w....................................	
h....................................	
c....................................	
k....................................	
f....................................	

d.................... **i**.................... **b**.................... **c**....................

What's the verb?

f....................

give

s....................

e....................

l............ eggs

what's the time please?

a....................

p....................

d....................

What's the adjective?

beautiful

w....................

c....................

c....................

e....................

What's the noun?

milk

b....................

w ....

l....................

s....................

e....................

b....................

f ....

m....................

p ....

f ....

f ....

i ....

2+2=4

TEST 10/10 ✓

Topic 14 Food matters

Food vocabulary;
elements in 'good' food;
calories

1 What's the word?

Vocabulary

1.1 Find the words

Can you find the names of the foods in the puzzle?
There are 12 words.

```
F  I  S  H  T  G  C  G  S  R  F  R  H  N  U
E  R  G  A  F  T  H  V  R  I  S  M  E  A  T
B  U  T  T  E  R  E  A  W  C  Q  V  N  M  H
I  D  O  R  J  U  E  U  I  E  O  P  L  M  D
C  E  R  E  A  L  S  S  U  Q  Z  E  G  G  S
B  E  R  D  F  G  E  J  S  W  Q  Z  X  D  F
R  E  M  F  H  K  V  P  O  T  A  T  O  E  S
E  R  I  T  I  G  F  R  U  I  T  L  I  P  N
A  Y  L  T  E  D  T  U  I  O  P  L  M  D  S
D  W  K  R  V  E  G  E  T  A  B  L  E  S  G
```

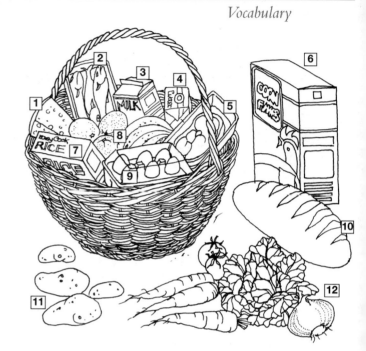

1.2 Label the food

This is what Peter eats on Saturdays.
Label the food. Say what is in each one. (See page 68 in your Student's Book.)

carbohydrate   fats   fibre   water   protein   minerals   vitamins

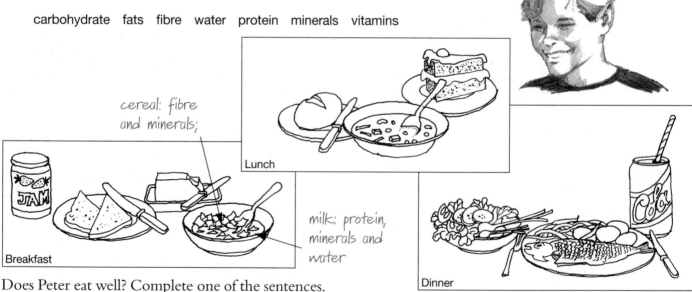

cereal: fibre
and minerals;

milk: protein,
minerals and
water

Lunch

Breakfast

Dinner

Does Peter eat well? Complete one of the sentences.

Yes, because ....

No, because ....

....

....

2 Talk to Linda

Write your answers to Linda's questions. Tell her about your lunch or dinner.

LINDA: Hello, how are you?

YOU: ....

LINDA: I'm fine. It's nearly time for lunch. Do you know what I have for lunch?

YOU: ....

LINDA: I have vegetable soup and fresh bread. It's delicious! What do you have?

YOU: ....

LINDA: Mmmmm, I like that too. How many meals do you eat every day?

YOU: ....

LINDA: I usually have three meals a day. Do you eat between meals?

YOU: ....

LINDA: Sometimes I have an apple or a biscuit. Oh, look at the time!
It's time to eat! Bye!

YOU: ....

📼 Talk to Linda on the cassette.

3 Read about food and energy

FOOD GIVES YOU ENERGY

It is important that your food has carbohydrates, fats, fibre, water, protein, minerals and vitamins. But it is also important that you don't eat too much or too little.

'Food gives you energy'
We talk about energy in calories

Calories per day

Boys		Girls	
9-11	2,200	9-11	2,200
12-14	2,650	12-14	2,150
15-17	2,900	15-17	2,150

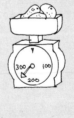

Look at the table.
How many calories do *you* need? ....

If Peter eats 45 g of cornflakes and 200 ml of milk, 75g of bread, 50 g of cheese, and a 150 g orange for breakfast, how many calories is that? ....

Find out how many calories you eat for breakfast, lunch and dinner in one day.

Different foods have different numbers of calories.

Cornflakes (30 g)	100	Chips (100 g)	180
Cheese (100 g)	300	Rice (100 g)	100
Chocolate (50 g)	250	Potato (100 g)	50
Fish (100 g)	100	Orange (100 g)	35
Bread (50 g)	150	Cola (100 ml)	250
Doughnut (100 g)	350	Milk (100 ml)	65

4 Complete the table

Every day, you use energy when you work, sleep, eat and play. Look at the clocks.

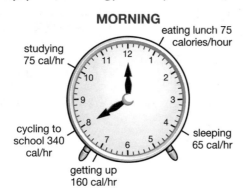

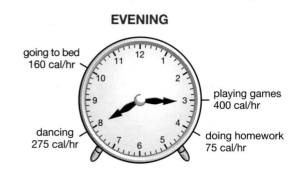

Think about your day. How many calories do you use?

For example:

Activity	Time	cal/hr	total
Sleeping	8 hours	65	520
Getting up	30 mins.	160	80
In class, at school	5 hours	75	375

Complete the table.

Activity	Time	cal/hr	total

5 Say it clearly!

Smile and say:

/iː/

Cheese

🔲 'Cheese' has a long /iː/ sound.
These words have the same sound. Listen.
Put a line under the long sound.

ch<u>ee</u>se   m<u>ea</u>t   sweet   eat   meal   week   beans   clean   teeth

🔲 Listen again. Now you say the words.

Say these sentences:

I like m<u>ea</u>t and ch<u>ee</u>se in my <u>e</u>vening m<u>ea</u>l.
I like to <u>ea</u>t sw<u>ee</u>ts.
I like to cl<u>ea</u>n my t<u>ee</u>th.

🔲 Listen to the sentences on the cassette.

6 Sing a song! I love chocolate

🔲 Look at page 155 in your Student's Book for the words to 'I love chocolate'.

Language focus

1 Choose the right sentence

Reading

Put sentences A–E in the correct place.
(See page 72 in your Student's Book.) What does Anne say?
Pat and Anne want to make shortbread biscuits.

PAT: OK. Have we got everything we need?

ANNE: [ ]

PAT: First, we need some sugar.

ANNE: [ ]

PAT: Good. And flour?

ANNE: [ ]

PAT: That's fine!

ANNE: [ ]

PAT: No, we don't. Butter. Is there any butter?

ANNE: [ ]

PAT: Not again! I know, we can make …

[A] Well, we've got about half a kilo.

[B] Butter. Er … Oh no! We haven't got any butter!

[C] I don't know. What do we need?

[D] We've got some milk and eggs. Do we need them?

[E] Yes. Yes. We've got lots of sugar.

Listen and check your answers.

Can they make shortbread? What can they make?

2 What have we got?

'some' and 'any'

2.1 Write some sentences

What's on the table? Look at the picture and write some sentences.

1 eggs – water *There are some eggs and there is some water.*

2 potatoes – meat *There are some potatoes but there isn't any meat.*

3 sweets – bananas ....

4 milk – sugar ....

5 cheese – fruit ....

6 butter – bread ....

7 rice – flour ....

2.2 Find the right bag

Write the correct letter A–D by each bag.

A In this bag, there are some potatoes, some eggs, some meat and some rice. There is also some sugar, some flour and some milk. There isn't any cheese.

B In this bag, there is some rice, some sugar, some butter and some bread. There is also some meat, some fish and some cheese. There isn't any water and there aren't any eggs.

C In this bag, there are some eggs, some potatoes, some bananas, and some sweets. There is also some water, some milk and some sugar. There isn't any butter and there isn't any bread.

D In this bag, there are some eggs, some potatoes, and some bread. There is also some rice, some butter, and some juice. There aren't any bananas and there isn't any meat.

1 ....

2 ....

3 ....

4 ....

3 Helen's dog

Object pronouns and possessive adjectives

Write the conversation in your language.

GIRL: Hello. ....

BOY: Hello. This is Helen's dog. Do you know where she is?

....

GIRL: No, I don't. ....

BOY: Do you know her telephone number? ....

....

GIRL: No, I don't. ....

BOY: Well, do you know where her brother is? ....

....

GIRL: No, I don't! ....

BOY: Do you know their house? ....

GIRL: No, I don't! ....

BOY: Well, I have their dog. Can you give them my telephone number?

....

GIRL: No, I can't! ....

BOY: Why not? ....

GIRL: Because I don't know Helen and I don't know you!

....

Talk to the girl on the cassette.

4   Say it clearly!   /e/

All these words have the same sound. Listen and say the words.

any   many   pen   when   ten   get   let   west   leg   egg

Say these sentences.

Have you got any eggs?   Can you get ten pens?   An insect has six legs.

5   Talk to Linda

Talking about likes and dislikes

Read Linda's questions. Then talk to her on the cassette. Listen to her music.

LINDA: Hello! How are you?

YOU: ....

LINDA: I've got a new cassette. Do you like music?

YOU: ....

LINDA: I like some types of music. Listen. This is my new cassette. Do you like it?

YOU: ....

LINDA   Oh no! It's the wrong cassette! This is my cassette. Do you like it?

YOU: ....

LINDA: I think it's really nice. Listen. This is my brother's music. What do you think?

YOU: ....

LINDA: Well, I don't mind it. Sometimes it's nice. He plays a lot of classical music. What's your favourite music?

YOU: ....

LINDA: Oh, yes. I like that too. I must go now. It's time to eat. Bye!

YOU: ....

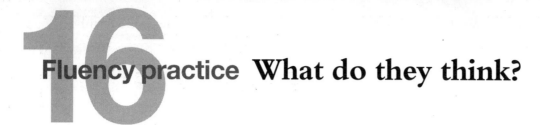

Fluency practice What do they think?

1 Which graph is correct?

Reading

Read the text. Which graph is it about?

FREE TIME

We asked 20 people what they do in the evening.

- Half of them stay at home.
- A quarter of them go out with friends.
- The other people do different things.
- Some of them play sports and some of them work or do other things.

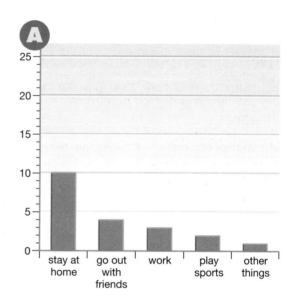

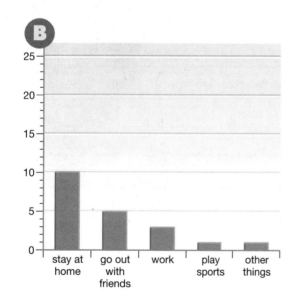

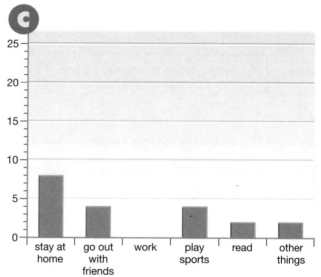

2 Write a description

Write a description of graph C.

We asked 20 people ...

3 Draw a graph

Read the text and draw a graph.

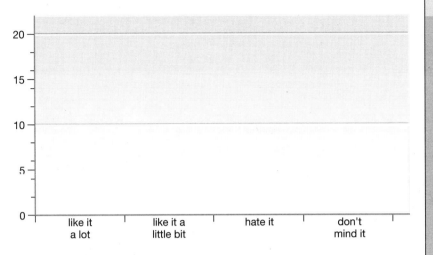

OUR TOWN

We asked 32 people what they think about our town.

● A quarter of the people say they like it a lot.

● Nine people say they like it a little bit.

● Four people say they hated it.

● The other people say that they don't mind it.

What did the biggest number of people say?

4 Write a questionnaire

You want to know about life in another country. What can you ask?

Some ideas:

the games children play   the food they eat   the weather

the plants and animals   the time people eat   the time people go to work

the time children go to school   when they have their holidays

Write some questions with possible answers. For example:

How many weeks' holiday do you have in the summer?

a two–three weeks
b four–five weeks
c five–six weeks
d more than six weeks

Write some questions without answers. For example:

What sports do most people play?

....

....

....

....

....

You can put your questionnaire in your *Parcel of English*.

17 Help yourself with vocabulary

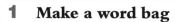

1 Make a word bag

1 Copy some new words onto cards.

2 Write the meaning in your language or draw a picture on the back.

3 Put the cards in a bag.

4 Take one out and test yourself!

> Cheese

Now you try it! Make cards with the words from the *Language Records* in your Student's Book. Put them in a bag and test yourself.

2 Make a jigsaw

1 Copy a text from your book.

2 Cut out some words.

3 Mix them up.

4 Put the words in the right place! Check your answers and do it again.

MONA: Hello. What's [ ] name?
SOPHIE: Sophie. What's your name?
MONA: Mona. Do you [ ] a sweet?
SOPHIE: Thanks.
MONA: Do you want to play volleyball?
SOPHIE: I don't know [ ] to play.
MONA: It's easy. I can [ ] you.
SOPHIE: OK. Let's go.
MONA: Where [ ] you live?
SOPHIE: In Prospect Street.
MONA: That's [ ] my house. Do you want to come to my house tomorrow?
SOPHIE: I don't know. I can [ ] my dad.
MONA: All right [ ] your telephone number?
SOPHIE: We [ ] got a telephone. I can ask him [ ] school.
MONA: OK.

Now you try it! Copy a text from Units 1–17 of your Student's Book.

Revision Life on Earth

Read about life on Earth. Complete the exercises.

Food; question forms

1 Find out! What is the population of your country?

Now:

....

10 years ago?

....

20 years ago?

....

Every day, the population of Earth gets bigger. In 1950, the population was about three thousand million (3,000,000,000). Now, it is about six thousand million (6,000,000,000) and it is growing faster. It is important that we look after the Earth. We need it!

The Earth gives us a lot of things. We also give the Earth a lot, but some of the things are not good.

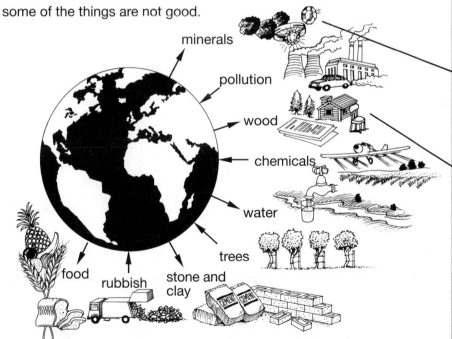

minerals

pollution

wood

chemicals

water

trees

food

rubbish

stone and clay

2 Write down three things near you now that come from

minerals:

....

....

....

wood:

....

....

....

In nature, when something dies, other animals and plants get food from it. Every animal or plant gives food for other animals or plants. Unfortunately, animals can't get food from many of the things that we 'give' the Earth. Animals, insects and plants can't eat metal, plastic and glass. These things will stay in the ground for many, many, many years.

3 Write down three foods that you eat that come from nature:

....

....

....

Look after the environment...

Some rubbish is very dangerous. It can poison plants and animals. Some animals eat plants. Some animals eat other animals. If one plant or animal dies, many animals can die.

4 If the grass dies, what happens to the fox?

....

....

....

Rabbits eat grass. Foxes eat rabbits.
What happens if the grass is poisonous?

In some places, many animals live together. One animal makes food for many more animals. If we put rubbish and chemicals in the water, the plankton can die. If there isn't any plankton, many animals have nothing to eat.

5 If the fish dies, what happens?

....

....

....

What can you do?

Don't leave any rubbish in the countryside!
Don't make so much rubbish!

6 If the plankton dies, what happens?

....

....

A picture dictionary (3)

Label the picture

s**weets**

r...............

b...............

f...............

v...............

p...............

j...............

f...............

d...............

e...............

c...............

b...............

m...............

m...............

f...............

What's the verb?

h**elp**

g...............

c...............

g...............

e...............

What's the noun?

m**eal**

b...............

b...............

l...............

d...............

t...............

b...............

e...............

b...............

s...............

h...............

What's the adjective?

n**ice**

f...............

e...............

s...............

b...............

h...............

19 Topic Into space

Space and the planets; pronunciation /eɪ/.

1 Star sentences

Reading, writing and vocabulary

1.1 Follow the numbers

Follow the numbers to make the sentences.

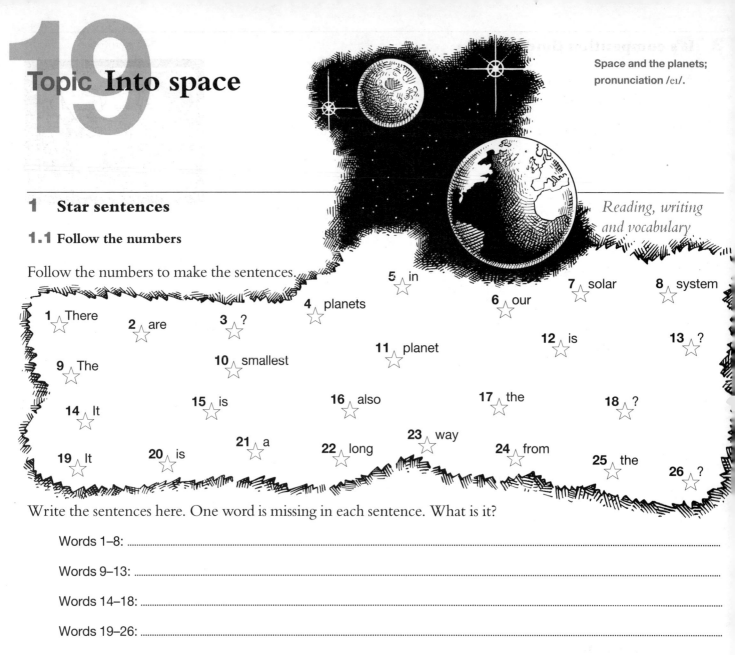

1 There **2** are **3** ? **4** planets **5** in **6** our **7** solar **8** system

9 The **10** smallest **11** planet **12** is **13** ?

14 It **15** is **16** also **17** the **18** ?

19 It **20** is **21** a **22** long **23** way **24** from **25** the **26** ?

Write the sentences here. One word is missing in each sentence. What is it?

Words 1–8: ....

Words 9–13: ....

Words 14–18: ....

Words 19–26: ....

1.2 Make a star puzzle

Find some short sentences in Unit 19 in your Student's Book.
Make a star puzzle for a friend or for your *Exercise Box*.

---

2 Right or wrong?

Reading and writing

If the sentence is wrong, put it right.

1 Gravity is weaker on the moon than on Earth. *True!*

2 Pluto is the hottest planet. *Wrong! It is the coldest planet.*

3 There isn't any air on the moon. ....

4 It takes millions of years for light to come from our nearest star. ....

5 The Earth is 75% water. ....

6 The sun and the moon are the same size. ....

3   It's competition time!

 You are on television. Listen to the cassette and answer the questions.

MAN: Welcome to Star Quiz! I have six questions for you.
Number 1. How many planets are there?

YOU: ....

MAN: OK. And my next question is: Can anything live on the moon?

YOU: ....

MAN: Excellent. Question 3. Why not?

YOU: ....

MAN: Yes. Because there isn't any air. Question 4. Why is the moon important
for ships?

YOU: ....

MAN: That's a difficult question! The moon makes the tides in the sea.
Two more questions. What is happening to the universe?

YOU: ....

MAN: That's difficult to understand. The universe is expanding. The stars are
moving. And now my last question. Question 6. Who were the first
people on the moon?

YOU: ....

MAN: Wonderful! Congratulations! Your prize is a trip to Planet Nevus for
two people!

4   Read Anne Brown's postcard

Reading

Anne Brown is an astronaut.
Read her postcard. Is she on
Planet Monz or Planet Kalip?

POST CARD

Dear Everyone,
We arrived here yesterday. It is
very beautiful. There are mountains
and rivers and small clouds in the
sky. We can walk outside and
breathe the air. There are some
small animals that live here. They
have eight legs and three eyes.
They are very nice. At this moment
they are making some food for us!

See you soon,
    Love
    Anne

5 Write a postcard

You are with Anne Brown. You are on Planet Nevus.
Write a postcard to your friends on Earth. Tell them
what you can see and what you are doing.

POST CARD

Dear everyone,
Here I am on Planet Nevus!
It is ....
I can see ....

....

There are ....

....

See you soon,

Love, ...

To ....

....

....

Planet Earth

6 Say it clearly!

/eɪ/

Listen. Say the words and the sentences. Open your mouth!

take   make   date   late   plate   hate   pancake

Light takes a long time to come from the stars.
The moon makes tides.
I hate pancakes!

7 Sing a song! Space

See page 155 in the Student's Book for
the words to 'Space'.

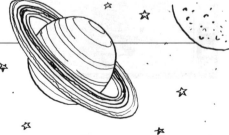

20 Language focus 1

1 The moon and tides

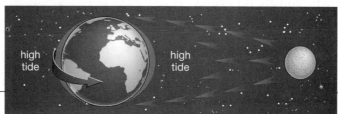

Reading

Match the texts to the correct pictures.

HOW DOES THE MOON MAKE TIDES?

A The moon helps to make tides. This is because the moon's gravity pulls the water.

B At the same time, the Earth is going around and around. Because of this the water moves out on the other side of the Earth.

C Because the Earth is going around, we also have two high tides every day.

D The moon also goes around the Earth. Sometimes the sun and the moon are pulling in the same direction. The sun also pulls the water. This means we have very high tides in some parts of the world and very low tides in other parts of the world.

2

3

4

2 What is she doing?

Present continuous

2.1 On the moon

Write a sentence for each picture.

1 <u>Anne Brown is opening the door.</u>

2 _____

3 _____

4 _____

5 _____

You are a TV reporter. Listen to the cassette and say what is happening.

2.2 What are they doing?

Write a sentence about each picture.

Your teacher has the answers.
Ask him or her next lesson.

*I think he's cleaning
something or opening a drink.*

---

3 Bigger or smaller?

*Comparatives and
superlatives*

1 COLD

Sweden is colder than France. Finland is the coldest.

2 TALL

David is .... Jane. Susan is the ....

3 STRONG

Susan is .... David. Jane is the ....

4 GOOD

David is .... Jane. Susan is the ....

5 BAD

Susan is .... David. Jane is the ....

> **Be careful!**
>
> **good–better–the best
> bad–worse–the worst**

4 In the bus station

Asking for travel information

You want to take a bus to Minton Town Centre
tomorrow afternoon. You want to know:

– the number of the bus
– what time the bus goes
– what time the bus comes back
– how much the ticket costs

You go to the bus station.
Listen and talk to the man.

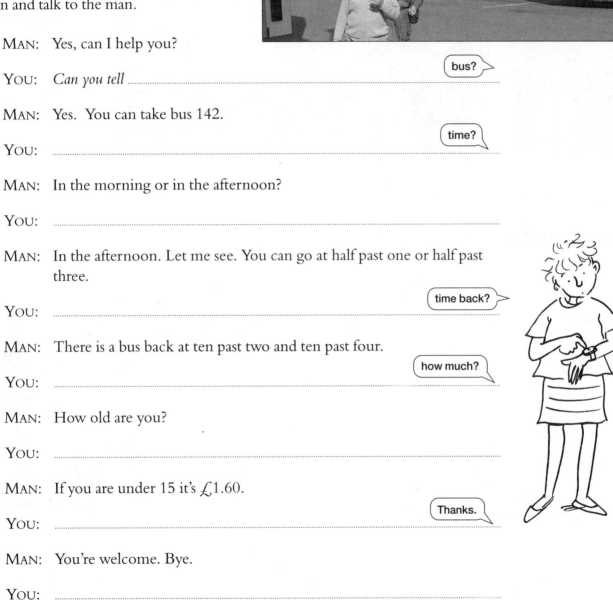

MAN: Yes, can I help you?

YOU: *Can you tell* .... **bus?**

MAN: Yes. You can take bus 142.

YOU: .... **time?**

MAN: In the morning or in the afternoon?

YOU: ....

MAN: In the afternoon. Let me see. You can go at half past one or half past
       three.

YOU: .... **time back?**

MAN: There is a bus back at ten past two and ten past four.

YOU: .... **how much?**

MAN: How old are you?

YOU: ....

MAN: If you are under 15 it's £1.60.

YOU: .... **Thanks.**

MAN: You're welcome. Bye.

YOU: ....

5 Say it clearly!

/ɪŋ/

Listen. Say these words and sentences with '–ing'.

opening getting coming putting starting waiting

He's opening the door. He's coming down the ladder. He's putting his foot on the moon.
I'm going to Planet Nevus tomorrow!

Fluency practice More poems from the Earth and space

Read a poem from space.   *Writing a poem*

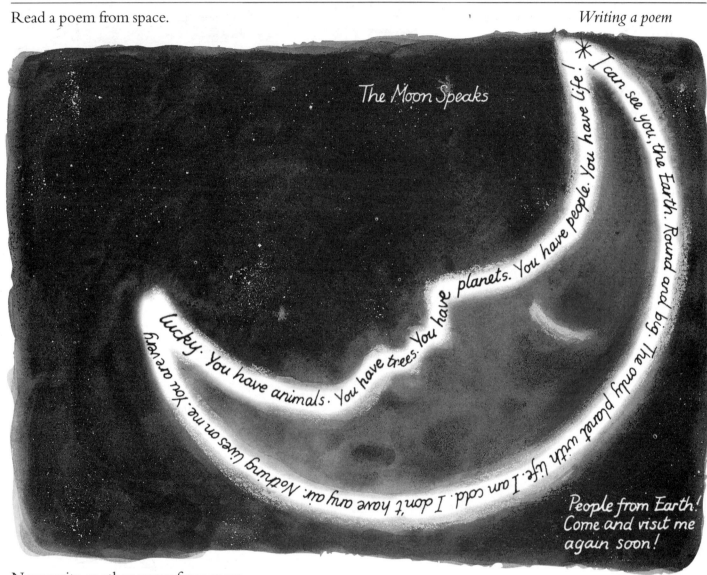

The Moon Speaks

I can see you, the Earth. Round and big. The only planet with life. I am cold. I don't have any air. Nothing lives on me. You are very lucky. You have animals. You have trees. You have planets. You have people. You have life!

People from Earth! Come and visit me again soon!

Now write another poem from space.

You can write about the moon, the sun, the stars, or imagine that YOU are in space.

You can use these ideas.

The moon speaks …   I am in space …
The sun speaks …   I am flying into space …
The stars speak …   Here I am on the moon …

I am hot.   I am cold.   I am millions of miles away.   I can see you.
I give you life.   I give you light.   I am history!

It is very dark.   There is nothing here.   I am travelling very fast.   It is very quiet.
I am alone.   It is very beautiful.   I don't like it here.   I like it here.   There are …
I can see …   I can hear …   I feel …   I am thinking …   I can't …

22 Help yourself with spelling (2)

1 Where are your mistakes?

1.1 Your mistakes

Look at your writing in English.
Make a list of your spelling mistakes.

1.2 Spelling groups

Put your spelling mistakes into groups:

Double letters	No 'e'
putting	driving
collecting	closing
ladder	leaving

1.3 PRACTICE

Now try it with these spelling mistakes.

Double letters	Vowels
hottest	animAL

1.4 Your writing

Now try it with your writing.

Unit 19 Ex 6

(sp) They're puting up a flag. He's *putting*
collecting
(sp) colecting rocks. He's drweing (sp) *driving*

a moon car. He's going up the
ladder
(sp) lader. They're closeing the door (sp) *closing*
leaving
(sp) They're leaveing the moon.

---

hottest
(sp) The hotest country in the

world is...
animal
(sp) The fastest animel in the

world is the...
biggest
(sp) The bigest building in the

world is the...
pyramids
(sp) The pyrameds in Egypt are

older than ...
planet
(sp) The nearest planit is...
getting
(sp) The space rocket is geting

closer to the moon.

2   Letter patterns

2.1 Letter patterns in English

Here are some letter patterns in English with 'e':

ea – near, sea   ei – protein, their
ee – see, street   eo – people

Here are some more letter patterns with 'h':

ch – chocolate, watch,   gh – high, neighbour
ph – geography, elephant   sh – shop, sheep
th – this, north   wh – which, who

Now look at a text in the Student's Book, for example
Unit 19, Exercise 4. Choose four letter patterns from
the list below. Try to find words for each pattern.
Look at other texts if necessary.

es ea th ff fr ere ai ay gh ol ng
ge ch ot ak ar is om nc

2.2 Some more letter patterns

Look at the *Wordlist/Index* in the Student's Book.
Choose four more words for each letter pattern.
Write the words on pieces of paper.

2.3 Play a game

You can play a game by yourself.

1 Turn the pieces of
   paper over.

2 Look at a word.

3 Test your memory.
   Find a pair of words
   with the same
   letter pattern.

1 What's the word?

Vocabulary

Here are some words from Units 19 and 20 in the Student's Book.
Put the letters in the right order and join them to the correct picture.

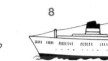

DXPNAE *expand*	PSHI	
GLFA	LPNETA	HTGIL ....
NOOM	YKS	SSRAT ....

2 The continents are moving!

Reading

2.1 A quiz about the continents

How many questions can you answer?

1 How many continents are there?
2 What are their names?
3 Something is happening to the continents. What?
4 Why are there mountains in the Himalayas?
5 What are earthquakes? Why do we have them?

2.2 Check your answers

Now read the text and check your answers.

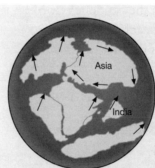

Millions of years ago, 'India' was not part of 'Asia'. India slowly moved north and then it hit Asia. This made the Himalayan Mountains.

135 million years ago

— THE CONTINENTS ARE MOVING! —

200 million years ago

Today, there are seven continents in the world but 200 million years ago there was only one! Asia, Africa, Europe, Antarctica, North America, South America and Australia were all part of one continent called 'Pangaea.' You can see on the map how the pieces go together.

Today, the continents are still moving! Australia is moving north, Africa is moving east and part of North America is moving west.

Present day

Millions of years from now, the world will be very different!

In many parts of the world today, there are earthquakes. This is because the land is moving.

2.3 Check your reading

Tick (√) the box to show if the sentences are right, wrong or if there is no answer in the text.

		Right	Wrong	No answer in the text
1	Two million years ago, there was only one continent.	☐	☐	☐
2	Europe is not moving now.	☐	☐	☐
3	There are nine continents.	☐	☐	☐
4	You can visit 'Pangaea' today.	☐	☐	☐
5	The Himalayas are in Europe.	☐	☐	☐
6	Millions of years from now, there will be 20 continents.	☐	☐	☐

SEE THE HIMALAYAS RISE!

Take two pieces of paper and make two balls. *Press the balls flat.* *Push them together.* Asia India *See the Himalayas rise!*

3 A quiz about the continents today

How many of these questions can you answer?

1 The biggest continent is ....

2 The coldest continent is ....

3 More people live in Europe than in Asia. Right or wrong? ....

4 The highest mountain in the world is in ....

5 The biggest rainforest in the world is in ....

6 Your country is in ....

7 The driest continent is ....

8 The smallest continent is ....

9 The biggest city in the world is in ....

10 The only continent without towns is ....

Look in your other schoolbooks or ask your friends and family for the answers.

A picture dictionary (4)

Label the picture

planet

s...............

E...............

'It .... 4½ years for light from the .... star to come to Earth.'

s...............

m...............

r...............

'G............... is very weak here.'

What's the verb?

jump

l...............

m...............

p...............

p...............

t...............

d...............

c...............

What's the noun?

ship

p...............

l...............

f...............

d...............

t...............

p...............

s...............

What's the adjective?

weak

s...............

h...............

c...............

h...............

l...............

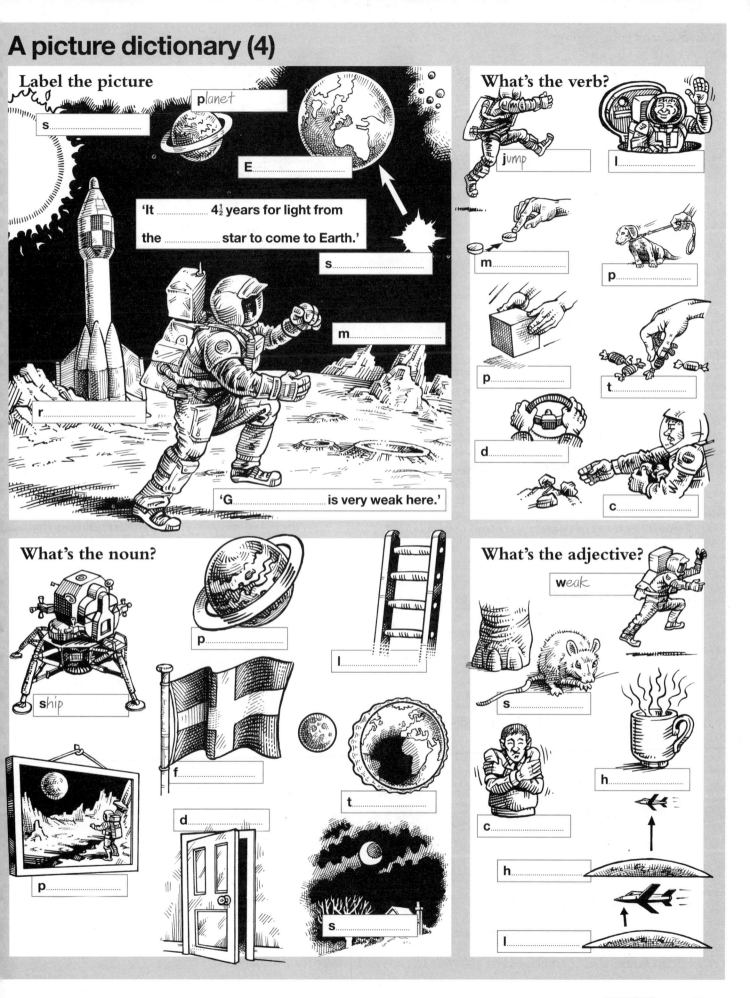

Topic 24 The weather

1 The months

Names of months

Find the names of 10 months.

```
N O V A M Z E A G J H
O F W T G H I P N A M
D E C E M B E R Z N A
A B W M A Y V I Y U P
Q R E X R J U L Y A W
Q U J O C T O B E R V
G A I L H U P F S Y Y
Q R B Y K J U N E T F
D Y O U A U G U S T S
```

Two months are missing.
What are they?

.... and ....

2 Read and write about the weather

Reading, writing and frequency adverbs

2.1 The south of England

Read about the weather in the south of England.

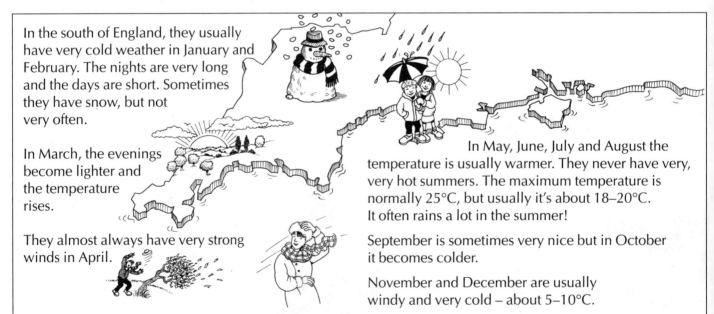

In the south of England, they usually have very cold weather in January and February. The nights are very long and the days are short. Sometimes they have snow, but not very often.

In March, the evenings become lighter and the temperature rises.

They almost always have very strong winds in April.

In May, June, July and August the temperature is usually warmer. They never have very, very hot summers. The maximum temperature is normally 25°C, but usually it's about 18–20°C. It often rains a lot in the summer!

September is sometimes very nice but in October it becomes colder.

November and December are usually windy and very cold – about 5–10°C.

2.2 Your country

Write about the weather in your country.

In January ...

3 What type of day is it?

Adjectives

🔊 Listen. Write down what type of day it is.

sunny   windy   chilly   foggy   rainy

a It's a sunny day.

b ....

c ....

d ....

e ....

Compare your answers next lesson.

4 Right or wrong?

Reading and writing

If the sentence is wrong, put it right. If you don't know, find out!

1 When a cold cloud meets a warm cloud, it makes rain.   *Right!*

2 Cold air rises.   *Wrong! Cold air falls.*

3 Lightning comes from static electricity in the clouds. ....

4 If you go up a mountain, you are nearer the sun. It becomes hotter. ....

5 Warm air falls. ....

6 Snow is very cold water. ....

7 Water is heavier than ice. ....

5 Fill in the words

Vocabulary

Fill in the words. What do they spell?

1 It's not hot. It's very ....

2 We breathe it.

3 June, July, ..., September.

4 The sun ....

5 In a cloud, there is .... vapour.

6 In Switzerland, they have a lot of ....

7 When a warm cloud meets a cold cloud, we have ....

8 The .... blows the clouds.

9 There is a very .... wind today.

6 Talk to David

Write your answers to David's questions.

DAVID: Hello. How are you?

YOU: ....

DAVID: I'm fine. It's very cold here today. What's the weather like with you?

YOU: ....

DAVID: Is it always like that at this time of the year?

YOU: ....

DAVID: Oh, really. Our winter is nearly the same as our summer. Are winter and summer very different in your country?

YOU: ....

DAVID: Tell me more.

YOU: ....

DAVID: That's interesting. I must go now. I'll talk to you again soon. Bye.

YOU: ....

Now talk to David on the telephone.

7 Say it clearly!   /ə/

Listen to how you often say '-er' in English. Say the words and sentences.

September   October   November   December
colder   hotter   drier   warmer

It is warmer in September than in October!

It is always colder in November.

It is never hotter in December.

We have the same sound in other words. Listen and say the words.

I have **a** dog at home.   How **are** you?   Lind**a** is **a** girl.

8 Sing a song! Singing in the rain

See page 155 in your Student's Book for the words to 'Singing in the rain'.

Language focus

---

1 The seasons

Reading

Do you know why they have the 'Midnight Sun' in some countries?
Do you know why we have seasons? Read and find out!

WHY DO WE HAVE SEASONS?

In many countries, there are seasons – spring, summer, autumn and winter.
When it is summer in the north, it is winter in the south.
When it is summer in the south, it is winter in the north.
Why? The answer is very simple!

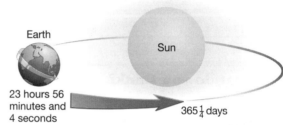

The Earth turns around in 23 hours 56 minutes and 4 seconds. This makes our day. The Earth also goes around the sun in 365¼ days. This makes our year.

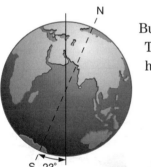

But the Earth is not straight! It has an angle of 23°. This means that only part of the Earth gets a lot of heat from the sun. This is the part nearest to the sun.

When it is summer in the north it is winter in the south.

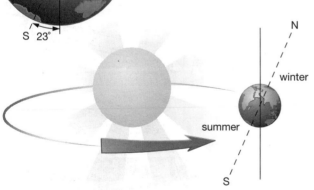

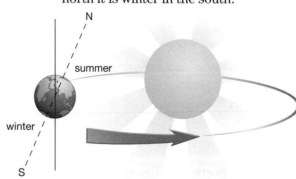

When it is summer in the south, it is winter in the north. The countries near the Equator have the same weather all the time.

In the winter, the places in the north and south get very little sun. It is night time almost all the time. In the summer, they get light all the time. They get the Midnight Sun!

Ask your family and friends if *they* know why we have seasons. Tell them if they don't know!

2 What's the word?

Put 'much', 'many', 'a lot' or 'a lot of' in each space.

'much', 'many',
'a lot' and 'a lot of'

3 What do you think?

Long comparatives and superlatives

3.1 Two cars

Look at these two cars. What do you think about them? Write some sentences with these words.

> exciting   expensive   long   comfortable
> beautiful   difficult to drive   fast   big inside

For example:

> I think the Sporty is more exciting than the Tuscan.

3.2 Three cars

Look at the Sporty and Tuscan again. Here's another car, the 'Adventurer'. What do you think about the three cars? Use the words in 3.1 and write a few sentences.

For example:

> I think the Adventurer is the most exciting.

Next lesson, compare your answers with the other people in your class.

4 What are you doing next week?

Making plans

Write down what you are doing next week. Write something on five days.

Monday...............................	Thursday...............................
Tuesday...............................	Friday...............................
Wednesday...............................	Saturday...............................
	Sunday...............................

Now talk to Linda on the telephone. She wants to go to the cinema on two days.

LINDA: Hi! How are you?

YOU: ....

LINDA: I'm fine. Listen. There's a new film called 'Adventures in Space 1'.
          Do you want to see it?

YOU: ....

LINDA: Wonderful! What are you doing on Monday?

YOU: ....

LINDA: Oh. Monday's a difficult day for me, now I think about it.
          What about Tuesday?

YOU: ....

LINDA: OK. There's another part of the film. 'Adventures in Space 2'.
          We can see that. What are you doing on Wednesday?

YOU: ....

LINDA: Wednesday. Oh no! I'm going to the dentist on Wednesday.
          Are you free on Thursday?

YOU: ....

LINDA: I'm going shopping on Friday. On Saturday morning I'm going
          swimming with my sister. After that, I'm free. When can we go to
          the cinema, then?

YOU: ....

LINDA: Great! That's fine. We can meet at my house at six o'clock. See you
          then. Bye!

YOU: ....

5 Say it clearly

/ɪə/ and /ɪəst/

Listen. Say the words and sentences.

sunny sunnier the sunniest   funny funnier the funniest
It's the sunniest day of the year!   He's the funniest person I know!

            happy happier the happiest
            This is the happiest day of my life!

Fluency practice

It's windy, sunny, rainy, foggy, chilly and cloudy in Australia!

1 What do you know about Australia?

Are these sentences true (T) or false (F), do you think?

a Sydney is the capital of Australia. [ ]
b Australia is bigger than England. [ ]
c Australia is in the Southern Hemisphere. [ ]
d They speak English in Australia. [ ]

e Australia has three different time zones. [ ]
f Australia is the smallest continent in the world. [ ]
g About 17 million people live in Australia. [ ]
h There are more sheep than people in Australia! [ ]

Your teacher has the correct answers. Ask him or her.

2 Read about Australia

Answer some more questions about Australia.

AROUND AUSTRALIA

Australia is a very big country. It is also the world's smallest continent. Look at the map and use your ruler.

How far is it from Perth to Brisbane?.................... kms
How far is it from Darwin to Adelaide? .... kms

Australia has everything. It has mountains, lakes, deserts, forests and rivers.

How many rivers can you find on the map? ....
rivers.
Which river is the longest?

.. .

Most of the people live in the parts where it often rains and where food can grow. This is in the south west and the south east.

Australia has snow, rain, strong winds and a lot of sun. Some parts don't get any rain or they get very little. In Darwin (*Can you find it on the map?*) the normal temperature is about 26°C in July and about 31°C in January. They get about 386mm of rain in January but they don't get any rain in July.

Is July in the winter or in the summer in Australia? ....

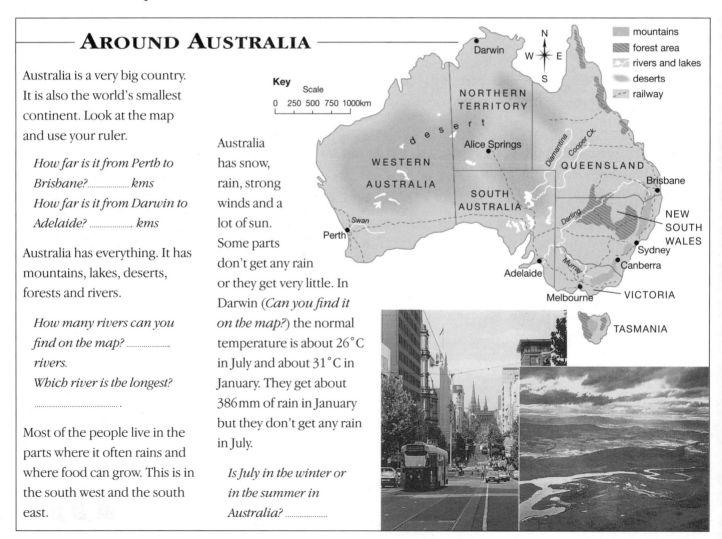

Key
Scale
0 250 500 750 1000km

mountains
forest area
rivers and lakes
deserts
railway

N W E S

Darwin

NORTHERN TERRITORY

desert

Alice Springs

WESTERN AUSTRALIA

SOUTH AUSTRALIA

QUEENSLAND

Diamantina   Cooper Ck.

Brisbane

Darling

NEW SOUTH WALES

Sydney

Canberra

Murray

VICTORIA

Melbourne

Swan

Perth

Adelaide

TASMANIA

In Melbourne, the weather is very different. (*Can you find Melbourne on the map?*) They get about 50 mm of rain every month. The temperatures are usually about 10°C (*In July or January?*) and 24°C (*In July or January?*).

Other parts of Australia are very hot during the day and very cold during the night. In the deserts, there aren't any clouds to stop the sun and temperatures rise to 52°C. The picture shows the Pinnacles Desert in Western Australia.

3   A postcard from David

Read this postcard from David.
He is on holiday in Australia.
Can you answer these questions?

- a Where is he? (Look at the map!)
- b What month do you think it is: January or July?

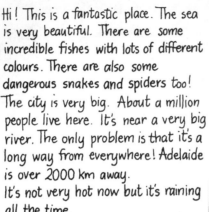

POST CARD

Australia
50c

Hi! This is a fantastic place. The sea is very beautiful. There are some incredible fishes with lots of different colours. There are also some dangerous snakes and spiders too! The city is very big. About a million people live here. It's near a very big river. The only problem is that it's a long way from everywhere! Adelaide is over 2000 km away.
It's not very hot now but it's raining all the time.
See you soon.
David

4   Write a postcard

Choose a place on the map and write a postcard.
Ask another student next lesson to guess where you are!

POST CARD

Australia
50c

27 Help yourself with pronunciation

1 Listen, look and repeat

Using a mirror

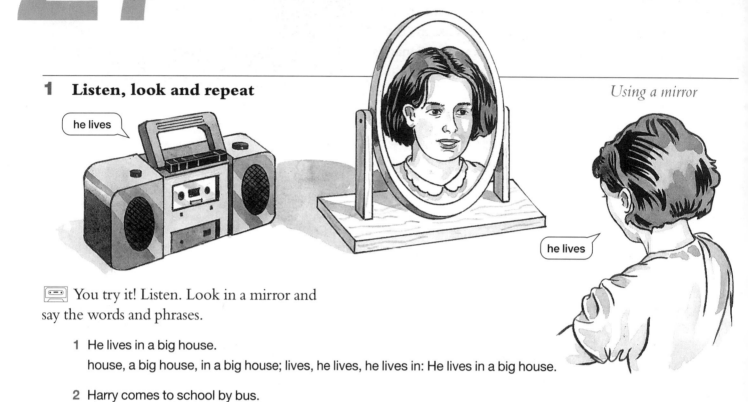

he lives

he lives

🖭 You try it! Listen. Look in a mirror and
say the words and phrases.

1 He lives in a big house.

house, a big house, in a big house; lives, he lives, he lives in: He lives in a big house.

2 Harry comes to school by bus.

bus, by bus; to school, to school by bus; comes, Harry comes: Harry comes to school by bus.

2 Bang on the table!

Stress in two-syllable words

2.1 Words with two syllables

Here are some words with two syllables.
The first syllable is the strongest.
Say the words and bang your hand on
the table when you say the first syllable.

London
writing jumping
hottest longer
kitchen teacher

London

__Lon__don   __wri__ting   __jum__ping   __hot__test   __lon__ger   __kit__chen   __tea__cher

🖭 Listen and say the words. Don't forget to bang the desk on the first syllable!

2.2 Some more words with two syllables

Look in the *Wordlist/Index* in your Student's Book.
Find some more two syllable words. Say them and
bang your hand on the first syllable.

parrot   **sea**son   **summ**er   **au**tumn

---

3   What are the important words?

Stress in a sentence

3.1 Important words

In English, we say the important words strongest. Like this:

SOPHIE: Oh NO. When ARE you FREE?

MONA: Well, FRIDAY is FINE.

SOPHIE: OK. We can have the party THEN. Can you tell ALI?

Listen. Say the dialogue.

3.2 Find a dialogue

Find a dialogue in your Student's Book.
Put a circle around the important words.

> SOPHIE: Barbara, are you free on Friday? After school.
> BARBARA: No, I'm not. I'm going to the dentist.
> SOPHIE: Oh, that's OK. What time?
> BARBARA: Four o'clock.
> SOPHIE: Can you come to my house after the dentist?
> I'm having a party.
> BARBARA: Great! Yes.
> SOPHIE: OK. Good. See you tomorrow. Bye.
> BARBARA: Bye.

3.3 Say the dialogue

Say the dialogue. Say the words in the circles stronger.

Listen to the dialogue on the cassette.
Do they say the words in the same way?

Well done!
Use the three ways to practise pronunciation in the
next units of the Workbook.

28 Test yourself

Here are some things you learned to do in Units 24–27.
How well can you do them?
Put a tick (√) in the box.

Now do this test and see if you are right!

I can do it:	very well	OK	a little
1 Talk about the weather			
2 Say how often you do something			
3 Compare things			
4 Making plans			

1 What's the weather like?

Adjectives and comparatives

Look at the pictures.
What can you say about the weather?

a

It's very windy!

b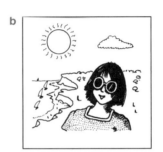

....

c

....

d

yesterday

today

....

e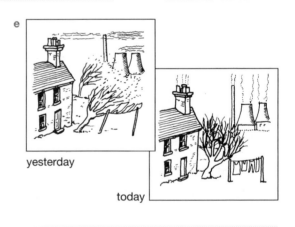

yesterday

today

....

2 How often do you do it?

Frequency adverbs

Write a sentence about each picture.

I always clean my teeth in the morning.

a

....

....

b

....

....

c

....

....

3 Talk about your country

Comparatives

Write your answers to David's questions.

DAVID: Hello. Can you tell me about your country? Is it bigger than Britain?

YOU: ....

DAVID: Oh. That's interesting. How many people live there?

YOU: ....

DAVID: Gosh! Is that more or less than Britain? I can't remember.

YOU: ....

DAVID: You know, my favourite season is summer. I like the long days.
Do you know, the sun doesn't set until nearly ten o'clock!
Is the day longer or shorter in your country?

YOU: ....

DAVID: Hmm. I don't like the winter very much. It gets dark so early.
It's dark at about half past three! Is it later or earlier in your country?

YOU: ....

DAVID: That's interesting. It's never very warm in Britain. In summer,
it's usually about 18°–20° and in winter it is usually about 5°–10°.
How is it in your country?

YOU: ....

DAVID: Listen. I want to play outside before the sun sets. Come on. Let's go!

Now talk to David.

4 Complete the puzzle

Making plans

Read the dialogue. Put the missing pieces in the correct place.

Pat: Hi, Anne! _____

Anne: Hi, Pat. What are you doing?

Pat: Well, _____ There's a new fun park in town.
_____

Anne: Yes! But when?

Pat: _____

Anne: No. I'm going to my uncle's house. What about Wednesday?

Pat: Wednesday? _____ I've got a music lesson.

Anne: _____

Pat: That's fine. What time?

Anne: Let me see. It opens at 10 o'clock and … Oh no!

Pat: _____

Anne: It costs £6 to get in!

Pat: What! Well, I can't go! _____

a What about Saturday morning?

b What?

c I haven't got any money.

d That isn't any good.

e It's Pat.

f Do you want to go?

g I'm reading a magazine.

h Are you free tomorrow afternoon?

A picture dictionary (5)

Label the picture.

cloud

t................... and
l...................

s...................

w...................

r...................

w...................
v...................

f...................

What's the verb?

meet

r...................

f...................

s...................

b...................

r...................

s...................

What's the noun?

air

t...................

g...................

i...................

What's the adjective?

high

s...................

w...................

c...................

h...................

r...................

w...................

s...................

29 Topic The cavepeople

1 What's the word?

Vocabulary

1.1 Find the words

Read the words and find the opposites.
Make an exercise like this for your class.

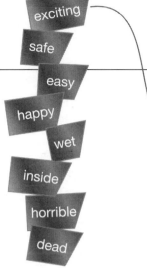

exciting safe easy happy wet inside horrible dead

alive outside difficult nice boring dangerous sad dry

1.2 A vocabulary puzzle

Read the clues. Write the words in the puzzle.

1 Cave life was exciting: it wasn't b.......................... .
2 Cavepeople went to s.......................... by the fire.
3 It was dangerous to s.......................... in the river.
4 Today we t .... by car, train and bus.
5 The m.......................... was the biggest animal the cavepeople killed.
6 I was b.......................... in 1975.
7 I was f.......................... on my first day at school.
8 I've got a sister but I haven't got a b.......................... .
9 Cavepeople killed animals with a s.......................... .

2 Write about the pictures

'was/were'

Write about Ngoba and her brother Mashan. Use 'was' and 'were'.

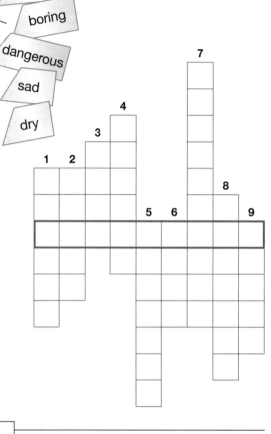

2 Ngoba and Mashan .... sad.

1 It ....

....

3 They ....

4 They looked at the animal.

5 It ....

....

6 It was easy to cut the skin.

7 They .... happy.

8 Ngoba and Mashan .... warm.

3 What did David do yesterday?

Regular past verbs

3.1 Write about David

Look at the pictures and write some sentences.

1 David cooked his breakfast yesterday.

2 ....

3 ....

4 ....

5 ....

6 ....

7 ....

3.2 What about you?

Write about what you did yesterday or last week.

4 A true story

Reading, writing and listening

Let's go this way today.

Where's Robot? I can't see him anywhere.

Look at this!

Fantastic!

Wow!

What's that?

🔊 Listen. The boys are telling a newspaper reporter about their adventure.

REPORTER: Hello boys. Tell me about your adventure yesterday.

MARCEL: Well, we went in the cave …

GEORGES: … suddenly on the walls on the first path there were lots of pictures …

SIMON: … first there were twelve elephants on one wall …

MARCEL: … and two on the opposite wall …

JACQUES: … then in the next path there were nine elephants on the wall …

GEORGES: … then three rhinoceroses …

SIMON: … five horses … and nine buffalo

JACQUES: … and at the end of the path there were eight more elephants and two more horses.

REPORTER: Good heavens! How can you remember all that?

JACQUES: We've got a map. Look. It's got all the animals on it.

REPORTER: Why are there so many animals in the same cave?

SIMON: The teacher said …

Draw the animals on the map.

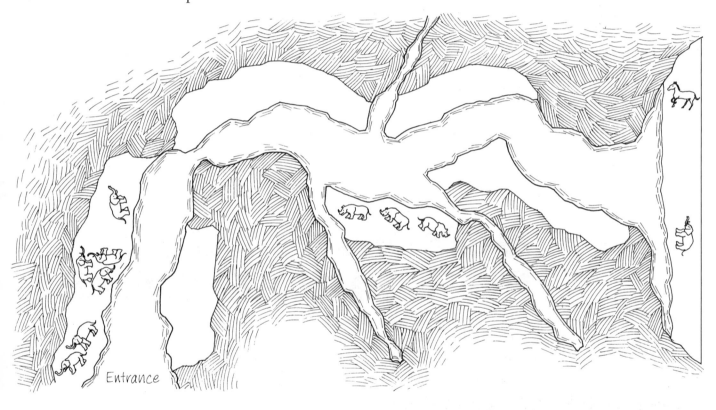

Entrance

---

5 Write the story

Writing

Write the newspaper story on a separate piece of paper.
You can use these sentences:

Four boys, Jacques, Simon, Georges and Marcel were friends.
In the summer of 1940 the weather was very hot. One day, …

6 Sing a song! Caveman rock

🔊 See page 155 in the Student's Book for the words to 'Caveman rock'.

30 Language focus

1 Word puzzles

Regular past tense verbs

1.1 Word puzzle

There are nine Past tense verbs in this puzzle.
Can you find them?
The words go down (↓), across (→)
and backwards (←).

```
L I S T E N E D
W A N T E D C E
D E P M U J R C
D E H S A W I I
X D R O P P E D
D E K L A W D E
L I K E D X X D
```

1.2 Your own puzzle

Make a puzzle for your friends. You can use these verbs.

  walked   talked   cried   watched   started   passed

Add some more of your own.

2 Colin's story

'was' and 'were'

2.1 Fill the gaps

Read the newspaper story.
Write 'was' or 'were' in the gaps.

BOY WAS LOST FOR THREE DAYS

Colin Becks, a teenager from Central High School, was alone in the woods for three days. He tells his story in his own words.

'Last Saturday there .... a big football match at the stadium. All my friends .... at the match. I don't like football so I went to the woods on my bicycle. It .... a very hot day. I stopped and had my lunch. Then I saw a hole near a tree. I went in the hole and into a big, cold cave. There .... two caves. A river went from the first cave to the second one. I decided to go into the second cave in the river.

Suddenly "BANG!". There .... a terrible noise. The stones from the wall filled the hole. They .... very big and heavy. I couldn't get out. After a long time, I went to sleep in the cave. I .... very tired. In the morning I decided to swim in the river to find the way out. The water .... very, very cold! I don't know how long I .... in the river, but it .... a long time! Suddenly, I saw the sun and the trees! I was safe!

2.2 A newspaper reporter interviews Colin

What did the interviewer say? Choose the correct question.

INTERVIEWER: Can you tell me what happened last Saturday?
COLIN: Well, I didn't have any friends to play with.

INTERVIEWER: ....
COLIN: Yes, they were. So I went to the woods.

INTERVIEWER: ....
COLIN: Yes, it was. I had my lunch and then I saw a hole under a tree.

INTERVIEWER: ....
COLIN: Oh very big. It went into a big cave.

INTERVIEWER: ....
COLIN: Yes. It was difficult to see. But there was a river on the left of the cave.

INTERVIEWER: ....
COLIN: I don't know! I decided to swim into the next cave.

INTERVIEWER: ....
COLIN: Yes, but when I was in the second cave all the stones came down from the wall!

INTERVIEWER: ....
COLIN: Yes I was! I decided to try and find another hole at the end of the river.

INTERVIEWER: ....
COLIN: About three hours I think. Suddenly I saw the sun and the trees! I was very happy!

a **How big was it?**
b **How long were you in the river?**
c **Was it deep?**
d **Were there two caves then?**
e **Were you frightened?**
f **Was it dark?**
g **Were they at the football match?**
h **Was it very hot on Saturday?**

Listen and check your answers.

3 Say it clearly!

/t/, /d/ and /ɪd/

There are three ways of saying '–ed' in English: a 't' sound (/t/), for example: washed
a 'd' sound (/d/), for example: lived
an 'id' sound (/ɪd/), for example: started

Listen. Say the verbs.

helped liked wanted decided asked stayed visited changed studied
looked watched played

Put the verbs in the columns.
Check your answers with the cassette.

Washed /t/	Lived /d/	Started /ɪd/

4 Some more about cave painting

Irregular past verbs:
'went', 'had', 'saw',
'ate'

Put the correct form
of the verb in the gap.

CAVE PAINTING

The cavepeople had different methods for painting.
They .... (have) five colours – black, brown, red, yellow
and white. Sometimes, they .... (make) pictures with
their hands and fingers. They also .... (have) paint
brushes. They .... (make) the brushes from small
bones and animal hair. When they .... (go) away from
home they painted on stones. The cavepeople usually painted
the animals they .... (see).

5 Talk to Linda

Talking about past
events

Write some questions for Linda and
some answers for her questions.

LINDA: Hi. Did you have a good weekend? I did. I went to the circus!   where?

YOU: ....

LINDA: It was in my town. It was here for two days. I saw the clowns.   funny?

YOU: ....

LINDA: Yes, they were. Then there were also some fire-eaters.   frightening?

YOU: ....

LINDA: Yes! Then we went home and had a barbecue. Tell me about a fun
weekend.

YOU: ....

LINDA: Oh! Were you with your friends?

YOU: ....

LINDA: Was there music?

YOU: ....

LINDA: Was there any nice food?

YOU: ....

LINDA: That sounds fun. I've got lots of homework now. Talk to you soon. Bye.

YOU: ....

📼 Now talk to Linda on the cassette.

31 Fluency practice Family trees

1 A family tree

🔲 Listen. Fill in the names and dates of birth on the family tree.

b. = born

Eva ═

Thomas ═ ....
died 1976

b. 19........

John ═
b. 19........

Jane
b. 19........

b. 19........

b. 19........

Amelia
b. 19........

"My name is Eva. I was a teacher but I don't work now. I was born in 1947. My husband's name is Thomas. He was a business man but now he likes to grow vegetables. He was born in 1933 in France. His first wife's name was Sally. She died in 1974. They had three children – Karen, Jane and Rachel. Karen and Jane were born in 1958 and Rachel was born in 1961 in London. In 1984 Karen married John. She works in a library and John is a doctor. He comes from Scotland. They have got two children. Charlotte was born in 1986 and Amelia was born in 1988. Jane works in a dress shop and Rachel is a pilot. She travels all over the world. We have got a daughter. Her name is Tara. She was born in 1985 in Bahrain."

2 What do they do?

🔲 Listen again. Can you write what each person's job is?

1 Eva *was a teacher but she doesn't work now.*

2 Thomas ....

3 Karen ....

4 John ....

5 Jane ....

6 Rachel ....

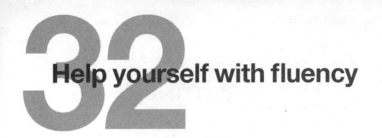

32 Help yourself with fluency

For this unit you need some cards, a cassette recorder and an empty cassette.

1 Phrases in the bag

Useful phrases

1 Write these phrases on some cards.

IN THE TOWN

About two kilometres from here.
There are some shops near the station.
There's a cafe near here.
This is the best cafe near here.

WHAT YOU THINK

I think so.
I don't think so.
I don't mind it.
I like it.
I hate it.
I think it's horrible.

THE WEATHER

It's hotter than yesterday.
It's a nice day today.
I was born in …?

2 Write them in your language on the other side.
3 Find some more phrases in your Student's Book and make cards for them.
4 Put all the cards in a bag.
5 Take out a card and translate it into English or into your language.

2 Talk to yourself!

Asking and answering questions

1 Record these questions on to your cassette.
(Wait a few seconds after each question.)

Hello, what's your name?
When were you born?
What school do you go to?
Where is that?
What's your favourite subject at school?
When did you start learning English?
Did you watch TV yesterday?
What did you watch?

2 Now talk to yourself! Play the cassette and answer your questions.
3 Find some more questions in your Student's Book and record them.

3 Have a conversation!

Good morning, how are you today?

Fine thanks, how are you?

Choose one of the situations below and talk to yourself.
Change your hat/chair/coat as you talk.

THE WEATHER IN YOUR COUNTRY

You 1:   What's the weather like in your country?

You 2:   Well, it's .... What's it like in your country?

You 1:   ....

YOUR SCHOOL TIMETABLE

You 1:   Hi. What do you think of the new school timetable?

You 2:   ....

You 1:   What's your ....?

You 2:   ....

YOUR TOWN

You 1:   Hi, where do you live?

You 2:   .... What about you?

You 1:   ....

THE ANIMALS YOU LIKE AND DON'T LIKE

You 1:   I've got a spider.

You 2:   Have you?

You 1:   ....

WHAT YOU DID YESTERDAY

You 1:   Hi, I went to the cinema yesterday. What did you do?

You 2:   ....

Use these three ways to help practise your English at home.

33 Revision Dinosaurs

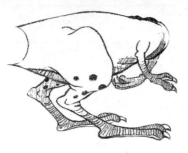

---

1 Words to revise

Vocabulary: nouns and adjectives

Here are some words from Units 29–32 in the Student's Book.

> exciting river wild
> wet poisonous life
> dark cave fruit soft
> dangerous
> deep jobs walls meat
> animals

Choose a noun and an adjective for each sentence.

1 The cavepeople lived an exciting life.
2 They lived in a ....
3 They killed many .... for food.
4 They liked to eat the .... first.

5 They painted pictures on the .... of the caves.
6 The children had to do some ....
7 They collected water from the ....
8 Sometimes they picked ....

📟 You can check your answers on the cassette.

---

2 Talk to Linda

Speaking

📟 Write your answers to Linda's questions. Then talk to her.

LINDA: What did you learn about in English this month?

YOU: ....

LINDA: Cavepeople! That's interesting! Did they have music like us?

YOU: ....

LINDA: That was clever! Did they have fire?

YOU: ....

LINDA: What did they eat and drink then?

YOU: ....

LINDA: Did the cavepeople live at the same time as dinosaurs?

YOU: ....

LINDA: You know a lot about cavepeople! I'm doing my maths homework now. Bye!

YOU: ....

3 When did the dinosaurs live?

210 million years ago   65 million years ago   15,000 years ago   today

Are these sentences true [T] or false [F]?

1 There were only 20 kinds of dinosaurs. ☐
2 Dinosaurs only lived in America and Africa. ☐
3 Some dinosaurs ate plants. ☐
4 They disappeared 65 million years ago. ☐

5 Dinosaurs were mammals. ☐
6 Birds come from dinosaurs. ☐
7 Some dinosaurs were bigger than a car. ☐
8 All dinosaurs had four legs. ☐

Now read the text below to see how many of your answers are correct.

Today there aren't any dinosaurs but for 75 million years more than 800 different kinds of dinosaurs lived all over the world. Some dinosaurs had two legs and some had four legs.

Most of them were very big; some were 30 metres long (the same size as a football ground) and weighed 30 tons (the same weight as three very big lorries). Some dinosaurs killed and ate other dinosaurs.

A brontosaurus

Many dinosaurs laid eggs in a nest and looked after their babies very well. The big dinosaurs moved very slowly – about 8 kilometres per hour – but the small ones ran faster.

The small ones were the same size as a chicken. Today's birds come from dinosaurs! They have the same kind of bones. 65 million years ago dinosaurs suddenly disappeared.

A tyrannosaurus rex

4 Make your own dinosaur!

Around the pages are different parts of four dinosaurs' bodies. Choose one of each part and trace it onto a piece of paper and make your own dinosaur. Give it a name and write about

– what it ate
– where it lived
– how big it was

A picture dictionary (6)

Label the pictures

cave

c.....................
p.....................

m.....................

s.....................

r.....................

s.....................

f.....................

a.....................

b.....................

b.....................

p.....................

b.....................

What's the past tense of the verb?

cooked

w.....................

s.....................

t.....................

p.....................

p.....................

h.....................

m.....................

p.....................

What's the adjective?

exciting

b.....................

h.....................

n.....................

d.....................

s.....................

h.....................

u.....................

h.....................

2 + 2 = e.....................

67269 x 17 = d.....................

What's the noun?

ice

h.....................

d.....................

s.....................

t.....................

l.....................

b.....................

c.....................

Language summaries

Units 1 and 2

'A' OR 'AN'?

You use 'a' with most nouns:

a book   a pen   a table   a car

You use 'an' with nouns that begin with a vowel sound (a, e, i, o, u):

an orange   an igloo
an orang-utan

'BE'

You can use 'be' in lots of ways:

– to say where someone is:

David is on a train.

– to talk about a person's job:

Susan is a teacher.

– to say how someone is:

I am cold.
Are you hungry?

– to say how old someone is:

He is 10 years old.

I am cold.

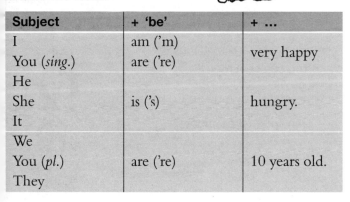

Notice the form:

Subject	+ 'be'	+ ...
I You (*sing.*)	am ('m) are ('re)	very happy
He She It	is ('s)	hungry.
We You (*pl.*) They	are ('re)	10 years old.

Negatives and questions are easy:

Subject + 'be' + 'not'	+ ...
I'm not (am not) You aren't (are not)	very happy today.
She He isn't (is not) It	here.
We You aren't (are not) They	hot.

'Be'	+ Subject	+ ...
Are	you	Peter?
Is	she	in America?
Are	they	hungry?

Are they hungry?

'HAVE (GOT)'

When you speak, you can say 'have got'.
(You can also say 'have' but 'have got' is more usual.)

I've got a new book.
She's got two brothers.
They've got short hair.

Notice the form:

Subject	+'have (got)'	+ ...
I You	've got (have got)	
He She It	's got (has got)	brown eyes. a guitar. long hair.
We You They	've got (have got)	

Negatives and questions are easy:

Subject	+ 'have' + 'not'	+ 'got'	+ ...
I	haven't (have not)	got	a sister.
He	hasn't (has not)	got	a bicycle.
We	haven't (have not)	got	English today.

'Have/Has'	+ Subject	+ 'got'	+ ...
Have	you	got	a big house?
Has	it	got	three heads?

PERSONAL PRONOUNS: 'I, YOU, HE, SHE' ...

I am a student.

You are a friend.

He is my brother.

She is my mother.

It is six today.

We are friends.

You are students.

They are my brothers and sisters.

'THERE IS / THERE ARE'

You can use 'There is ' and 'There are' to say that something exists. The subject usually comes after 'There is' and 'There are':

> There are a lot of kangaroos in Australia.
> There is a river in my town.

You say 'There is' for singular nouns and things you can't count (see **Theme E**):

> There is a park in my town.
> There is some sugar on the table

You say 'There are' for plural nouns:

> There are a lot of tall buildings in New York.
> There are 650 students in my school.

PLURALS

You can make the plural of most nouns with 's':

> a pen ➡ two pens   a dog ➡ two dogs

Some words are different:

> child ➡ Look at those children!
> foot ➡ He's got big feet!

Words that end in '-y' change to '-ies':

> country ➡ There are many small count**ries** in Europe.
> baby ➡ Look at those bab**ies**!

Words that end in '-f' often change to '-ves':

> leaf ➡ The lea**ves** on the trees are brown.

'CAN'

You can use 'can' in four ways:

1 You can say what you can or can't do:

> She can play the trumpet very well.
> I can't play the piano.

2 You can say if something is possible or not:

> You can buy milk in that shop.
> You can't eat metal!

3 You can ask if you can do something:

> Can I open the window?

4 You can ask for something:

> Can I have a drink of water, please?

Can I have a drink of water, please?

Notice that 'can' is followed by the infinitive without 'to' and is the same for everybody:

Subject	+ 'can'	+ Infinitive	+ ...
I You (*sing.*) He She It We You (*pl.*) They	can	play go	football. home now.

Theme A

PARTS OF SPEECH: NOUN, VERB, ADJECTIVE

A **noun** is a name of a person, place or thing:

    a girl   a school   a table

A **verb** is an action word:

    run   eat   ride   swim

An **adjective** describes a noun. Notice that the adjective goes *in front of* the noun:

    a **big** flat   a **new** bicycle   **short** hair

PRESENT SIMPLE: POSITIVE

You can use the Present simple to talk about:

– something that happens regularly:

    I come to school by bus.

– something that happens generally (or always):

    He lives in a flat.

Notice the form. Notice the '-s' with 'he', 'she' and 'it'!

Subject	+ Present	+ ...
I You We They	live drink	in a small town. a lot of milk.
He She It	live**s** drink**s**	in a big house. a lot of milk.

PRESENT SIMPLE: NEGATIVE

You can make a negative sentence with 'don't' ('do not') or 'doesn't' ('does not') *after* the subject. ('Have' and 'be' are different! See pages 89 and 90.)

Subject	+ 'don't/ doesn't'	+ Infinitive	+ ...
I You We They	don't	live swim eat	in a flat. in the sea. meat.
He She It	doesn't	play watch sleep	football in the park. television at home. at night.

It doesn't sleep at night.

Theme B

PRESENT SIMPLE: QUESTIONS WITH 'DO' OR 'DOES'

Questions in English often use the verb 'do'. You can use questions with 'do' or 'does' when you want to ask about:

– something that happens regularly:

    Do you go to bed before 9 o'clock?
    Does your mother work on Saturdays?

– something that happens generally (or always):

    Do you live in a big town?
    Do elephants eat meat?
    Does your brother come to this school?

Notice the form. 'Do/Does' is *before* the subject. The main verb is *after* the subject:

	'do/does'	+ Subject	+ Infinitive (without 'to')
What	do	elephants	eat?
Where	does	a shark	live?

Notice when you say 'do' and when you say 'does':

'Do'	+ Subject	+ Infinitive	+ …
Do	I you we they	have eat sleep	brown eyes? fish? a lot?
Does	she he it	have eat sleep	brown eyes? fish? a lot?

You can also put a question word at the beginning:

> **When** do bats sleep?
> **Why** does a giraffe have long legs?
> **How** do birds know the way home?
> **How long** does an elephant live?
> **What** does a shark eat?
> **Where** do pandas live?

You can give a short answer with 'do' or 'does':

Do I have brown eyes?	Yes, you do. or No, you don't.
Does he eat fish?	Yes, he does. or No, he doesn't.

POSSESSIVE ADJECTIVES: 'MY, YOUR, HIS, HER', ETC.

Possessive adjectives are words that say who something belongs to.
They come *before* the noun:

> This is **my** dog.
> **His** horse is very old.

Subject	Possessive adjective	Example
I	**my**	Where is my dog?
you (*sing.*)	**your**	What's your name?
he	**his**	That's his house.
she	**her**	Her horse is very old.
it	**its**	The cat sleeps in its basket.
we	**our**	This is our pet crocodile.
you (*pl.*)	**your**	Where is your mother?
they	**their**	Cows give milk to their babies.

You can also make possessives with names of people or things by adding 's:

> This is Pat**'s** house.
> That's the dog**'s** food.

Theme C

'SOME' AND 'ANY'

You use 'some' and 'any' when you talk about a quantity of something:

> Have you got any money?
> There are some eggs on the table.

Usually you use 'some' when you say **positive sentences**:

> I have some water in my cup.
> They want some butter for the shortbread.

You use 'any' with **questions**:

> Do we need any milk?
> Have you got any salt?

You also use 'any' with **negative sentences**:

> Oh no! We haven't got any sugar!
> We don't need any butter.

OBJECT PRONOUNS: 'ME, YOU, HIM, HER', ETC.

Object pronouns are words for the object of an action. They come *after* the verb:

Subject	Verb	Object pronoun
This is my bedroom. I	like	it.

Subject	Object pronoun	Example
I	**me**	Can you help me?
you (*sing.*)	**you**	I can see you!
he	**him**	Do you know him?
she	**her**	I can telephone her.
it	**it**	Do you like it?
we	**us**	Good food is important for us.
you (*pl.*)	**you**	These books are for you.
they	**them**	Vitamins are important. You need them!

Theme D

PRESENT CONTINUOUS

You can use the Present continuous when you want to talk about something that is happening *now*.

Notice the form:

Positive:

Subject	+ 'be'	verb + '-ing'	+ …
He	is	coming down	the ladder.
They	are	flying	into space.

Questions:

'Be'	+ Subject	+ Verb + '-ing'	+ …
Is	he	driving	the moon car?
Is	he	opening	the door?

Negatives:

Subject	+ 'be' + 'not'	+ Verb + '-ing'	+ …
She	isn't	wearing	a sweater.
The sun	isn't	shining	today.

You can also use the Present continuous to talk about plans and definite events. See *Plans* page 95.

COMPARATIVES AND SUPERLATIVES (1)

You can compare things by putting '-er' and '-est' at the end of adjectives that have one syllable, such as 'long, tall, big, near, fast, old, hot, small':

Adjective	Comparative	Superlative
long	longer	the longest
tall	taller	the tallest
big	bigger	the biggest

You use 'than' after the comparative form ('longer than …'), *never* 'that'!

Mercury is hott**er** than the Earth.
The Sun is **the** hott**est** thing in the solar system.

Pluto is small**er** than Mercury.
It is **the** small**est** planet in the solar system.

Notice small ⟶ small**er** ⟶ **the** small**est**
BUT hot ⟶ hott**er** ⟶ **the** hott**est**

Notice some irregular adjectives:

Adjective	Comparative	Superlative
good	better	the best
bad	worse	the worst

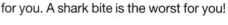

Maths is good for you. History is better for you. English is the best for you!
A dog bite is bad for you. A snake bite is worse for you. A shark bite is the worst for you!

Theme E

COUNTABLES AND UNCOUNTABLES

In English, you can count some nouns but you can't count some other nouns.
You can say:

Five apples. Three tables. Six bags of sugar.

These nouns are 'countables'.

You **can't** say:

~~Six sugar.~~ ~~Four snow.~~ ~~Seven water.~~

These nouns are 'uncountables'.

'MUCH', 'MANY' AND 'A LOT OF'

You use 'much' for uncountables in questions and negative sentences:

Do you have much work tonight?
How much milk do you have?

We don't have much sugar.
They don't have much rain in Saudi Arabia.

You use 'many' for countables in questions and negative sentences:

Do you have many brothers and sisters?
How many eggs do we need?

I don't have many friends here.
She doesn't have many ideas.

For positive sentences you can use 'a lot of' for uncountables and uncountables:

We have a lot of green hills in England.
He has a lot of money in the bank.

COMPARATIVES AND SUPERLATIVES (2)

You use 'more …' and 'the most' to compare adjectives with more than one syllable.

> This car is **more** expensive **than** that car. This car is **the most** expensive.
>
> I think swimming is **more** exciting **than** walking.
>
> Windsurfing is **the most** exciting sport for me!

Adjectives that end with '-y' change to '-i-':

> It is very wind**y** today. It's much wind**ier** than yesterday.
>
> He looks happ**y**. He's the happ**iest** man I know!

Theme F

PAST SIMPLE

You use the Past simple to talk about something at a definite time. For example, 'yesterday', 'last night', 'in 1993' and so on.

PAST SIMPLE: 'BE'

The Past simple of 'be' is 'was' or 'were':

> Where were you last night?
>
> I was on another planet!

Notice when you use 'was' and when you use 'were':

Subject	+ 'be'	+ …
I		at the football match on Saturday.
He	was	in my house yesterday.
She		at a party last Sunday.
It		10 years old last month.
We		on holiday last Wednesday.
You	were	at school last week.
They		ill yesterday.

PAST SIMPLE: REGULAR VERBS

Most verbs are regular. They all have '-ed' on the end:

> I **walked** home from school yesterday.
>
> We **watched** a horror film last night.
>
> They **washed** the car yesterday.

PAST SIMPLE: IRREGULAR VERBS

Some verbs do not use '-ed'. They are all different:

> I **went** to bed at 6 o'clock on Sunday.
>
> I **made** a cake yesterday.
>
> I **saw** Peter last Thursday.
>
> I **had** a lot of homework last night.

PAST SIMPLE: QUESTIONS AND NEGATIVES

Regular and irregular verbs use 'did' to make questions and negatives.
Notice the form:

'Did'	+ Subject	+ Infinitive	+ …
Did	he	go	to a party last week?
Did	you	watch	TV last night?

Subject	+ 'didn't'	+ Infinitive	+ …
I	didn't	like	that film.
She	didn't	go	to school yesterday.

SHOPPING

You can ask for things in shops:

MAKING FRIENDS

You can talk about yourself and ask someone about themselves:

I live in …   Where do you live?

My telephone number is …   What's your number?

My name's …   What's your name?

INVITING

You can ask someone if they want something or if they want to do something:

Do you want a biscuit?

Do you want to play football?

Do you want to come to my house?

LIKES AND DISLIKES

You can talk about what you like and don't like:

Do you like …?   Yes, I do.
No, I don't.

I think it's/they're   horrible.
beautiful.
boring.
interesting.

I think it's horrible.

ASKING FOR TRAVEL INFORMATION

You can ask about times and ticket prices:

Can you tell me which bus goes to the zoo?

What time is the bus?

What time does the bus come back?

How much is a single ticket?

How much is a return ticket?

PLANS

You can ask about plans. You can use the Present continuous to talk about plans:

Are you free on Saturday?

Can you come to my house tomorrow?

What are you doing tomorrow?

I'm going to the dentist on Monday.

She's having a party on Saturday.

They're doing their homework tonight.

TALKING ABOUT PAST EVENTS

You can use the Past simple to talk about something in the past:

Last summer ...   Last week ...   Last night ...
I went to ...   I saw ...   I had ...   I played ...
I made ....

You can ask questions about the past:

Was it nice?

Was it exciting?

Were you with your friends?

Was the food good?

Was it a birthday party?

Was there music?

Acknowledgements

The authors and publishers are grateful to the following illustrators and photographic sources:

Illustrators: Sophie Allington: pp. 27, 28*b*, 30*l*, 33, 34*tl*, 37*t*, 39, 50; Felicity Roma-Bowers: pp. 29*l*, 32*b*, 58; Maggie Brand: pp. 40*t&b*, 41*b*, 43*b*, 51; Robert Calow: pp. 4, 10, 13*m*, 44*t*; Richard Deverell: pp. 49*m*, 61*t*, 64*b*, 79*t*; Hilary Evans: pp. 15, 17*tr&br*, 20*b*, 22*bl*, 24*ml*, 25; Gecko Limited: all DTP illustrations and graphics: pp. 7*b*, 8, 9*t*, 14, 18*t*, 21*m*, 22*br*, 25, 29*tr&mr*, 30*r*, 32, 33, 34*tr*, 41, 42*t*, 46, 47*t*, 49, 50, 53, 54, 58, 61*b*, 67, 70, 71, 75, 77*t*, 80, 82; Peter Kent: pp. 11, 21*b*, 26, 44*b*, 45*t*, 68*b*, 74, 76, 89, 90, 91, 93, 94, 95, 96; Steve Lach: pp. 19, 24*mr&b*, 35, 36, 48, 53*b*, 54*t*, 59, 60, 72, 73, 84, 85; Jan Lewis: pp. 6*t* , 12*m*, 14*b*, 16*m*, 24*t*, 25, 28*t*, 32*tr*, 42*m*, 43*t*, 47*b*, 57, 62, 64*t*, 65, 66*m*, 69*b*, 80*t*, 81; Colin Mier: pp. 31, 32*tl*, 34*b*, 56*b*, 82*b*; John Plumb: pp. 12*t*, 13, 25*br*, 83; John Richardson: p. 23; Debbie Ryder: pp. 6*b*, 13*b*, 29*b*, 42*b*, 54*b*, 66*b*, 79*b*; Chris Ryley: pp. 5, 7*m*, 12*b*, 16*t&b*, 17*tl&bl*, 18*b*, 22*t*, 32*m*, 37*b*, 38*t*, 40*m*, 41*t*, 45*b*, 66*t*, 69*t*, 75, 77*b*, 78, 82*t*, 86, 87, 88; John Storey: pp. 7*t*, 52, 53*t*, 55, 63, 68*t*.

Photographic sources: The J. Allan Cash Photolibrary: pp. 70, 71, 80; Biophoto Associates: p.38; Nigel Luckhurst: pp. 9, 56, 57.

t = top   *m* = middle   *b* = bottom   *r* = right
c = centre   *l* = left

Picture research by Sandie Huskinson-Rolfe of PHOTOSEEKERS.